Questions
of
Religious
Truth

Wilfred Cantwell Smith

QUESTIONS

OF

RELIGIOUS

TRUTH

CHARLES SCRIBNER'S SONS · NEW YORK

PREFACE

Religiously concerned men today face new questions, without knowing quite what they are.

Many who for a time felt the traditional religious affirmations to be false, are no longer sure that the matter is quite that simple. Many who all along felt that they were not false, are yet restless. Both groups have come to sense that the classical forms may have expressed a legitimate and serious, even valid, awareness, but no longer express it felicitously or even perhaps effectively. Venerable doctrines reflect a reality that one guesses may be or feels sure is still there while the doctrines somehow may not now reflect it. The sensitive man is left feeling that the traditional religious answers are to questions other than those in which he today is personally involved.

This series of lectures is an attempt to raise new sorts of question. It does so not in the thought that these are precisely the issues with which modern men are engaged. On the contrary, these are unwonted queries, provocatively strange. They are pressed here in the hope that by turning to novel issues and by treating old problems in novel ways, it may be possible to illuminate the area out of which the old questions once arose and out of which also the new will eventually be formulated. It is the task of the theologian to articulate in words the vision to which men of faith legitimately aspire. By probing in new directions, as here, it is hoped to contribute to that endeavour.

Because our first chapter treats the "death of God" movement, let it not be supposed that our concern is sensationalist or with ephemerals. Because our second chapter raises the question, Is the Qur'an the word of God? let no one imagine that this is a book about Islam. More accurately, let no one but a Muslim imagine that. It is a book about religious truth: about where men have found it in the past, and where conceivably we may hope to find it today, or at least where it may be reasonable to look for it, and what kind of thing it may be that we are looking for.

The material here presented was delivered first as the Taylor Lectures for 1963 at Yale Divinity School, except the opening chapter which is part of a Charles Strong Memorial Lecture delivered in the Australian universities in July 1966. The Islamic material was submitted also to a Muslim audience at the Jamia Millia Islamia, New Delhi, in 1964, and chapters two to four to a partly Christian-missionary, partly Hindu audience in Jabalpur that same year under the auspices of the Henry Martyn Institute of Islamic Studies. I am grateful to the Rev. Mr. Ian Douglas and the Board of the Jabalpur institute for their cordiality; to Principal Mujib and his colleagues for their unfailing interest (without Muslim as well as Christian involvement I would not venture to make public these ideas); to Mr. C. R. Badger and the other Strong Trustees for their thoughtful arrangements and hospitality; and especially to Acting Dean Forman of Yale and his colleagues not only for acting as gracious hosts and for encouragement but also for their original invitation to make my first public appearance as a theologian.

In this published version the lecture form has, at the instance of the publishers, been thinly disguised ("last evening's talk" has become "the preceding chapter," and the like). Yet the fact that the last three chapters were conceived for an explicitly Christian audience and delivered before other religious groups has left its mark: I have been able to take certain matters for granted and to leave certain concepts unexplained, in the confidence that these religious groups would understand. To elaborate them now, or to expound the same positions in vocabulary more familiar or more persuasive to a public with other starting points, would have burdened these pages unduly and robbed the argument of whatever pithiness it may possess. Normally I strive to write in such a way that secularists as well as men of overt faith, and Buddhists as well as theists, may find the theses intelligible, even cogent. Any published "we" that refers to a community less than mankind, I usually find unsatisfactory. In the present case I trust that others may accord an interim tolerance while I attempt to make a point in a form that is specifically and explicitly theological. I find myself hoping that they may perhaps even have sympathy for the point, if not for the form. Yet having been invited, as a Christian, to speak before a Christian group, I have done so to the best of my ability.

W. C. S.

CONTENTS

I   THE "DEATH OF GOD"?

The "Death of God"?

Anyone who would give serious attention to the recent movement in the United States that has made quite a splash by calling itself a Christian atheism, must first face a few preliminary questions. Does it deserve serious consideration? Might one not better give heed to, let us say, the early Buddhist movement? It also has been called atheist, and for twenty-five hundred years now has provided men and women in the millions with a life, whatever their beliefs, of deep faith, of evident richness and transcendence, of conspicuously and rewardingly religious quality. It would seem not difficult to argue that, in comparison, this new movement not only is less tested but also is less disciplined, less rational, less powerful, less serene; certainly less lovely and less wise. Or should one rather consider the faith that for long some men have surely had in secular humanism, a movement with its prophets and its martyrs; and ponder what may be involved in such faith, and also nowadays in a possible loss of it?

Is there not a danger, in the "death of God" case, of succumbing to a trick of provocation? Even the protagonists of the movement, and certainly the rest of us, must guard against an exaggerated even if innocent attention to the spectacular as such, giving ear simply to the strident.

13

Just as the neon signs of modern street advertising become more and more blatant, more and more grotesque, to attract, each more than the last, our attention and to wheedle our dollar, so here one wonders whether it is perhaps the sheer appearance of stark outrageousness that attracts notice. Once it has done so, then that fact can itself attract more notice; and so it goes, in our fad-ridden age. I should perhaps confess that I am not altogether sure about an answer to this. The movement seems important not primarily because of what it is saying theologically, but because of the response that it is eliciting sociologically. Yet is that response genuine?—or is it largely sensationalist and nourished by such facts as that the popular press publicizes it and that many of us hustle to analyse and to interpret it? I have decided to run the risk; guessing that for all its potential spuriousness, the movement is important—for good or ill. Moreover, and more cogent, the matter is worth attention because if we can contrive to understand it we shall have taken a significant step toward enlarging our apprehension of human religiousness.

There is certainly a great deal that one might say in response to the writings of this group—whether in explanation or in criticism: might say as a theologian, as a twentieth-century intellectual, as a philosophic critic, and in other capacities. I will confine myself, however, to making some remarks as an historian of religious movements, noting this new emergence as a development within the total context of the history of man's religiousness and the variegated pattern of its expression.

Perhaps before doing this I must defend myself on

another score, in view of the fact that some, at least, of these thinkers object to being called, or having their ideas called, "religious." This I feel need not be taken seriously. They like to call themselves Christian, but not religious. This derives historically from the Barthians, and psychologically in part from a rather sorry self-righteousness which supposes that one can avoid, or claims that one is avoiding, the faults that manifestly mar other men's comparable enterprises. To hold that other men are "religious," and to disdain them for it, while one's own group is superior (because it has, rather, "faith"; or because it is world-affirming; or whatever) is not merely much too simple a way of dealing with the beam in one's own eye. More important is that, in calling attention to the motes in other people's, it is in danger of almost denying that they have eyes, or at least that they can see. When they say, "Other men are religious, but we are not," they mean that they judge others to be less intelligent, less honest, less modern, than themselves. I do not mind too much that such a device arrogantly over-estimates oneself—we have got used to that in the religious field. My complaint is that it under-estimates one's fellow. The failure to appreciate the value, and the validity, of other men's religiousness is far too serious to be lightly perpetuated and reinforced.

These men, then, I would insist, are religious, and theirs is a religious movement. In fact, the most fundamental point that must be made about the "death of God" notion is that this phrase must be understood and can only be understood as a religious symbol. If I can somehow manage to convey what I mean by that assessment, my task will be virtually done. Much of the confusion arises from attempting to take these words in some other way, as if they were plain prose and meant what they seem to say. Both the theology and the movement make sense, I would submit, if one keeps this religious interpretation firmly in mind; and fail to make sense if one does not.

What, then, is meant by saying that the phrase functions for them as a religious symbol; and indeed, as an ultimate religious symbol? First, it is sacred; and second, it is therefore translucent. Those for whom it is sacred, when they look at it do not, like the rest of us, see it, but see through it to something beyond—something not precise, not objective, not finite. It is not something that they see, perhaps, so much as something about which they feel—and feel deeply. Its form serves as a highly charged crystallizing of whatever emotions or insights or sense of ultimacy it can be made to carry for those who treat it as absolute.

To understand it—just as to understand the syllable *OM* for Hindus, or the Qur'an for Muslims, or any myth —one must ask oneself how much transcendence it can be made to carry for those who have chosen its particular shape to represent the pattern of their religiousness. The sacred must always be not only ambiguous but unlimited: it is a mystery, so that no specific significance can exhaust it—there is always more waiting to be explored. A religious symbol is successful if men can express in terms of it the highest and deepest vision of which they are capable, and if in terms of it that vision can be nourished and can be conveyed to others within one's group.

A religious symbol does not, then, have its meaning in itself. A cross, for instance, means nothing to a Muslim;

and no amount of examining crosses will help him to learn its religious significance. You can listen to the syllable *OM* until you are blue in the face, but that will never in itself lead you to hear in it what the Hindu hears. One must try to discover what the Hindu hears in it: or better, hears through it. (A beginner's step in studying the history of religion is to realize that the Hindu, again, does not revere the cow that we see, but the cow that he sees. . . .) Admittedly, some progress towards understanding symbols can be made if one asks not what does the symbol mean, simply; but rather, what does it mean for the particular men who use it religiously. Fundamentally, however, even this must be transcended; one must think of the symbol in terms not of its meaning something, but of its focusing or crystallizing what *life* means, what the universe means, to those who through this symbol find that life and the universe can be seen (or felt) to *have* coherent meaning.

The "death of God" phrase, accordingly, does not mean anything in itself. For the non-believer, it is an absurd juxtaposition of terms. And even for its devotees, it, and even the mythical event to which it allegedly refers, do not prosaically mean something specific, but rather shimmer with a whole cluster of potential meanings— meanings deep and vibrant, which they find not in the phrase but in life, and then hear echoing in the phrase with some reverberating ultimacy.

It is not difficult to illustrate this orientation in the proponents of this movement. And once one approaches it in this manner, one finds that it all begins to make sense. For Thomas J. J. Altizer, for instance, who is the most

17

scintillating of the writers, the "death of God" is clearly not a conclusion to which he comes but, quite explicitly and decisively, a starting point. This is where we must begin, he and his friends loudly affirm, and loudly reiterate [1].

Secondly, that it is symbolic rather than ordinary language is evinced in that the phrase resonates with more hidden connotations than even those who use it can apprehend. Altizer and another protagonist, William Hamilton, introduce their latest collection of writings, a kind of joint manifesto, with these confessions: "Radical theology . . . best interprets itself when it begins to say what it means by that phrase. The task of clarifying the possible meanings of the phrase, 'death of God,' is scarcely begun." [2]

Indeed, they then list suggestively a wide spectrum of ten possible meanings, which are not even logically compatible with each other, and are not meant to be. Furthermore, they assert that what they and their writings have in common, in the midst of much diversity, is—and this language is highly interesting—a "response to the death of God." In fact, the whole movement could best be described just so: a response to this symbol ("event," they call it—symbolic event, if you will). In other words, the

[1] Many references could be given for this. For example: "We shall *simply assume* the truth of Nietzsche's proclamation of the death of God" (Altizer, in Thomas J. J. Altizer and William Hamilton, *Radical Theology and the Death of God,* Indianapolis, 1966, p. 95); theology, if it is to be modern, "must *first* assess the theological significance of the death of God" (id., ibid., p. 11) (italics are ours).

[2] *Radical Theology and the Death of God* (Indianapolis, 1966), p. ix.

18

phrase is not like other phrases (prose phrases, that is), a device for conveying meaning with as much precision as possible from one human being to another; rather, it is like other religious symbols, something to which the religious life is the response (and, one may add, of which the meaning becomes gradually available, *after* one has responded).

As a religious symbol this phrase, this three-word myth, is in some ways totally new. This fact in itself gives it some considerable saleability, psychologically and otherwise, among some in the modern world. The emergence of radically powerful new symbols in man's religious life is an interesting thing to watch. In an earlier day we would have said that we were witnessing here the birth of a new religion. We *are* witnessing, I am sure, a new religious movement being born. When Nietzsche used the phrase, for him it was a kind of prose; or of poetry, but not religious poetry. To offer it as a religious symbol, as something around which faith can cluster, around which the imagination and the emotions can play, by which the subconscious can be stirred, to which life can be organized as a response—this is strikingly new.

The elements out of which it is composed, however, are not new. Both prongs of this paradox, one discovers, are historically important.

First, there is death, which prehistoric archaeology would suggest has served as about the oldest and most persistent, as it is the most widespread, of religious symbolisms. Men's capacity for a religious orientation to the world has everywhere been stimulated and evoked in life by life's mortality. By death, even those who may not be affected by any other religious symbol will sometimes dramatically, vividly, even if but for a moment, be lifted from a mundane to a religious attitude to life.

Secondly, there is "God," which in the Western tradition religiously has been a verbal symbol par excellence. The name with its subconscious connotations is necessary to endow the rejection with the appropriate emotional and psychological charge.

Thirdly, although not as a phrase, the death of God as an event on Good Friday has, of course, been a Christian symbol of stupendous consequence. An historian of religion would be much more surprised to hear of a new religious movement arising out of the midst of, let us say, the Muslim world using this particular symbolism than he is out of the Christian.

Nonetheless, I do not mean to undercut the novelty of this perhaps almost chance creation. Part of the emotional power of the new constellation derives, I am sure, from traditional associations. Another, explosive, part, however, clearly derives from the very negation of tradition: the garnering in under a religious aegis of emotions and ideas that manifestly had been accumulating *against* the traditional religious associations. And it is this combination that has triggered the new explosion.

The juxtaposition of the words "death" and "God" seems to outsiders absurd; but for those for whom it has become religiously significant, the very act of bringing together these two polarities has resulted in the emitting of a whole shower of sparks, emotional and in some cases even intellectual. And from these sparks some fires have been lit, to burn through the walls of the purely mundane, making openings through which they have again caught sight of a transcendent realm from which they had previously felt themselves shut in. My own guess here is that unconsciously—without being either willed or understood—a series of such reactions was let loose in the psyche of these men; and it is proving that that experience can be and is being repeated by others. A psychologist of religion is confronted here with a spectacular case study of the power of a new social symbol.

The question, then, is not what does the phrase "death of God" mean; and especially not what does it mean to those of us on the outside. It is rather, what can men, consciously or unconsciously, make it mean once they have adopted it as a final symbol, have surrendered to its transcendent potentialities—or we may better say, have surrendered to it their transcendent potentialities.

First, let us recognize that those for whom it is helpful are especially men who in our day are bewildered by the lostness of their living, the collapse of their traditions, the strangeness of their opportunities and challenges. And it is particularly that kind of person, of whom in America there are millions, who in a confused and perhaps desperate way would like to be a Christian but cannot believe, or who feels that he ought to live a Christian life but no one will tell him how.

Our problem then is to see to what use such men could put a symbol of this kind, emotionally and even intellectually, and even spiritually. Phrased in that way, the question is not difficult to answer. Let us look at some of the meanings to which this symbol lends itself.

First, it can express, and sanctify, the sorrow and

poignancy of a loss of faith. Those for whom the old symbols no longer convey meaning, and who sense therefore
that something rich and valuable has gone out of their
lives, can express their loss through this symbol, and de-
clare its seriousness. In a sense, they can thereby give
their despondency a cosmic significance. An ordinary
atheist is left feeling, presumably, that he and his society
were simply wrong, deluded; and he must cheerfully
make do with and even prize the bleakness of a life from
which this quality, this color, this dimension have been
lost—whereas these men can regret their loss, and affirm
that it is a real one. Almost they can feel that the universe
itself somehow takes seriously their desolation.

Yet the symbol can express not only despondency but
also hope. I mentioned the Good Friday parallel. Not with
all, but evidently with some, there are echoes of that here;
so that it is possible even while bemoaning the loss of the
divine to feel that maybe eventually there may yet be a
resurrection. Men whose experience or insight does not
enable them to share in the triumphant joy of the Christian who lives this side of Easter, through this new symbol
can yet live, as it were, in the interval between Good Friday and Easter; so that although they do not have joy,
they may yet have hope.

One detects a certain sense of men waiting for something to happen; or at least of their leaving the door open,
just in case it might.[3]

---

[3] Traditional theologians and preachers have lamentably failed to convey to modern men the symbolic truth and power of Easter, even its
symbolic meaning, once it has become apparent to many that it is not
literally true (nor, literally, even significant).

In addition to despair and hope, the symbol can serve also, however, for anger. And of this one discerns a good deal. The movement is one of revolt—we shall return to this presently—and also of resentment. There is a bitterness because the old order has passed, the old symbols have failed one; and a resentment against fathers and against society generally because of one's sense of deprivation and loss. Again in contrast to an old-fashioned unimaginative atheism, this myth allows one to take oneself seriously in one's feeling of having been let down, not only by other people but almost by the universe itself. By it, both pity and protest are given a cosmic status.

The symbol is open, moreover, to serving the purposes of action, of responsible moral behavior and social dynamic. In fact, one of the chief uses to which its spokesmen put this myth is to portray, and again to sanctify, to render cosmically serious, the new moral responsibilities with which man finds himself, because of modern science and technology. It is possible to make "the death of God" notion mean the God has died, even deliberately and as it were self-sacrificingly, in order to hand over to man the responsibilities that He, God, used to carry: creativity, the guiding of history, responsibility for human destiny. What others of us using traditional Christian vocabulary would express by stressing the immanence of God along with or more than the transcendence, or by saying—as I myself, for instance, did say some years ago—that in modern times God has actually become more immanent in human history than He used to be in earlier centuries, these men express by saying that God has died, handing over to man the role of arbiter and architect of the future.

It is possible to represent to oneself that an acceptance of this new symbolism is to take on (not like a traditional atheist, whimsically, but dutifully, because it has been bequeathed) the task of being up and doing, committing oneself to the responsibility of ordering the world. Again, there are echoes here of the doctrine of the Incarnation.

It is even possible for some to develop a new kind of Unitarianism: of the three persons of the Trinity, they would discard the Father and the Holy Spirit, but retain the Son. They can call themselves Christians because they take the man Jesus, whom they even call Christ (though I think that that is cheating a little), as a kind of model for moral behavior, for all men. There are echoes here of the classical saying of Athanasius: God "became man, in order that we might become divine" [4]—or perhaps they are revising this to read, "God became man, in order that men might become modern" (or perhaps, "modern Americans"?).

There are echoes not only of the Incarnation and *Kenosis* doctrines but also of Amos and Isaiah, and of course of the Social Gospel. That the business of the Christian is not merely liturgical, but is to accomplish something in the workaday world, to play a responsible and constructive role in secular affairs, is of course nothing new in Christian thinking; but these men are saying it in a novel and iconoclastic way.

[4] *De Incarnatione,* 54:3. The verb used, *theopoiēthōmen,* might be translated "might become gods," or, "might become God"; or, over against modern anthropocentric distortions of what is involved in this miracle, one might insist on "be made" rather than "become." Cf. also Irenaeus, *Contra Haereticos,* Liber V, praefatio; Origen, *Contra Celsum,* 3:28.

These last remarks bring us to a consideration of the relation of this myth to traditional Christian symbolism; and it is time to turn to that.

For it is all very well, whatever may be said about the potentialities, or even achievements, of this myth in itself, in isolation. There is still, however, the point of its violent colliding with the whole of Christian history. This, of course, is crucial; and there are several matters to be remarked here.

The first is that, as already commented, this is a theology, or shall we say ideology, of revolt. Now I should like to draw attention here to a matter that I deem of some seriousness. In the past, all atheism in the West has in effect been in the name of Greece, against Palestine. It is the rationalist, the philosopher, who has argued that religion is false: reason versus faith. From a world perspective, one can recognize, as I have elsewhere argued, that the famous Western controversy has been inaptly named. More accurately, one should see it as a debate not between reason and faith, but between a faith in reason and a faith in God; or, more historically, between faith through the Greek heritage of Western civilization, and faith through the Judaeo-Christian heritage. The standard Western position has comprised the two faiths [5] together, whether in tension or in balance; but occasionally persons have arisen to argue that they are incompatible, so that men must have only one. Now the great dénouement of the twentieth century has been that faith in each of the two traditions has petered out. Many artists and novelists and thinkers have lost not only faith in God, but faith in

[5] At its best, the double-channeled faith.

reason. They see behind the flux of phenomena neither an ultimate Person, creator, redeemer, judge, nor a rational order, a meaningful cosmic structure in relation to which, and in terms of which, meaning for human life can be formulated. Metaphysics is in even more total collapse today than is theology. Modern philosophy departments in general, and linguistic analysis in particular, are what is left of the philosophic tradition, once those practising it have lost their faith in a transcendent truth.

And indeed, we have to do in this new movement not merely with a loss of faith but with an active revolt—against ontology and rationalist ethics, against the intellect (logos) as an interpreter either of what is, on a cosmic scale, or of what ought to be.

Not only have the philosophy departments in a modern university largely abjured their erstwhile role as a guide to man's understanding of himself, his destiny, or his universe. In addition, the "death of God" theologians even go so far as to represent their own rejection of the idea of God as a rejection of philosophy, of Greece, in the name of a revival of, or truer reading of, Jesus and the Bible and of Palestine.[6] (That this is historically inaccurate does not bother them particularly; they sit rather lightly by history.) The revolt is also against the Jewish-Christian tradition in Western culture, against the Church; but it is almost as if the suggestion were being put forward that the mistake that the Church has made these two thousand years in believing in God has been due to a false under-

[6] Cf. Altizer, "Nirvana and Kingdom of God," reprinted in *New Theology No. 1*, Martin E. Marty and Dean G. Peerman, edd. (New York, 1964), p. 152.

standing of the universe foisted upon it—by the pressures, one might almost say the rape, of Greek thought.

The revolt against the Greek spirit in modern Western culture, though considerably less noisy and less commented upon than that against religion, is perhaps no less significant and may prove no less consequential.

In the "death of God" movement there is more of repudiation than this, however. The revolt is valued in itself, in what looks like an adolescent frenzy. Those not caught up in it stand a little aghast at the sheer exuberance of destructive hostility that is a striking and even applauded characteristic of much modern Western, and not least American, life: where the teenager is almost assured that there must be something neurotic about him if he does not hate his parents; and in the peculiarly American tradition, the violence of revolution can appear as almost sacred in itself. The following passage was written by perhaps the humblest and gentlest of the spokesmen, William Hamilton: "We must rebel against the father, and against everything for which the father is a symbol: the past, tradition, authority as coercive, even religion and the church. As we have already seen, some of us may even need to rebel against God, to accuse him of injustice or impotence or irrelevance, in order to come to know him. Rebellion of this kind may be the only way of being honest with ourselves, and for many in our time it will be the only way religious faith can come, if it can come at all. Rebellion against the father can be a means of self-knowledge and of the knowledge of God." [7]

[7] William Hamilton, *The New Essence of Christianity* (New York, 1961), pp. 140–41.

This movement is the theological version of the Angry Young Men.

Iconoclastic movements in religious history have had many facets. Forms and images can be destroyed in the name of something higher, which they are thought no longer to exemplify; or in the name of something lower, when what they stand for is misunderstood or ignored; or simply in the name of destruction itself, since some people like to smash things, idols included. The historian of religion knows a whole gamut of rejection: all the way from the *via negativa* of the mystics, of which one can detect some signs here, to—alas—sadistic impulses attracted to or even perhaps generated by iconoclastic drives. The destruction of the temple of Somnath by Mahmud of Ghaznah was pious, but was no pretty sight.

The inebriated delight in Bonhoeffer's phrase, "a world come of age," with its arrogant narcissism, is relevant here. The phrase is innocent enough, and all of us know quite starkly what lies behind it. The self-satisfied delight in the phrase, however, and particularly the delight taken in batting over the head with it all who would draw different inferences from the same facts—this self-assured belligerence is not altogether sober. The fierceness of anti-traditionalism is surprising to those of us who more quietly feel that we came of age some while ago, and more humbly feel that the next generation, and the next century, will probably know a good deal more than we do, and may even be wiser. To have come of age is not necessarily to have become infallible.

On the contrary: in the realm of the understanding of human religiousness and its ideas, including the variegated history of the idea of God, we are just beginning to approach the kind of comprehension that induces humility rather than confident generic pronouncements. So far as religious ideas are concerned, that man has not come of age in the modern world who cannot yet use symbols, or reject them, with some sophisticated and diffident sense of the complexity of the relation between the particular and the general in this realm—and hence some undogmatic sense of multiformity. Caution and exploration are what is modern.

This ideology, on the other hand, is like other traditional evangelisms and orthodoxies—religious, classical Freudian, classical Marxist—in that it too has a glib and devastating method of explaining away in its own terms, and therefore dismissing without taking seriously, any position that differs from its own. The device in this case involves, for one thing, a concept of the "authentically modern," or "genuinely contemporary." Having posited that their view is the right one for today, these men can dismiss any other as not modern; at least, not "authentically" modern, as Altizer calls it.[8] (They apparently do not notice that the concept of authenticity here is metaphysical. There is the curious inconsistency that otherwise modernity is supposed to be characterized by diversity, even chaos; yet they feel sure that there is one, and only one, religious ideology or attitude that is right in this situation.)

Why anybody would wish to be authentically contemporary, it is difficult to imagine. Personally, because of my knowledge and appreciation of the past, and because of

[8] Hamilton is much gentler here.

my vision of the future, I transcend the present—as well as because of my faith in God, my sense of the quality of transcendence itself, in others, in me, and in the world. As I study human history, I find no one whom I can admire who did not transcend his own age, *his* contemporaneity. And not only those I admire; but rather, all men. The capacity to transcend one's time and place is part of what it means to be a human being. Woe unto modern men who are merely modern! [9]

Perhaps further helpful in understanding this movement is the recognition that there is, especially in the United States, a curious hatred of the Church among churchmen, and a curious sense of guilt lashing out. One does not at all know whether men in this modern mood actually feel more guilty than do other peoples, or whether perhaps they are fighting their way through to a liberation from a guilt that others of us keep more firmly repressed. Certainly the hatred of (an ill-understood) Puritanism seems emotionally violent. One also suspects that there may be perhaps among Church leaders a guilty

[9] "Authentically contemporary" is one of Altizer's again symbolic phrases, serving a religious purpose for him (so that in arguing against it one is in effect saying that his ideals are not high enough, as well as contending that he is being too disdainful of those who prefer other symbols). There are others. One is "dialectical": he uses this exuberantly —and dismisses Tillich's theology, for example, on the grounds that it is "only partially dialectical" (Altizer and Hamilton, *op. cit.*, p. 107), as though this were quite trenchant. Another term used apparently as some kind of ultimate, is "eschatological"—a term that he even equates with "non-religious" (*e.g., ibid.*, p. 153), which to a non-believer in his system is quite ludicrous (and especially to an historian of religion). We on the outside must strive to recognize that of such terms an entire symbol system is privately constructed which to the person who uses it reverently is coherent and final.

conscience about the Barthian aberration, especially its rejection of culture.

However that may be, one cannot but be struck by the self-righteousness of this new group. This has been characteristic enough of other religious movements in the past, of course; but one had hoped that we had moved beyond this. The "death of God" phrase, as we have said, means many things to its proponents; but one of the things that it has meant is the death of the idea of God (though it is a rather cheap trick to confuse the two). On inquiry, it would seem that as usual it is other men's idea of God, at that, that is being castigated. I find myself surprised at the insensitivity and discourtesy, to say the least, with which they berate the religious views of those from whom they differ—and as usual, whom they misunderstand and underestimate as well. The evangelists of this new movement remind one, for all the world, as they lash about within Christendom, of the evangelistic missionary of more orthodox type who turned up in India and China in the nineteenth century, and feeling quite sure that his own Christian vision was the right one, and that the gods of the superstitious natives were at best idols and at worst demons, affirmed his own faith in terms of the falsity, and the destruction, of theirs.

In fact, the specifically missionary spokesman of this new movement, the European van Leeuwen, expresses this cultural and theological aggression against the rest of the world more or less explicitly.[10] The radical displacement of all other religious systems by the new Christian

[10] Arend Th. van Leeuwen, *Christianity in World History* (London, 1964; New York, 1966).

secularism is confidently and complacently postulated. And just as the old missionary was at times in alliance with the guns of imperialism, so the new explicitly allies himself with the dominating forces of modern technology, which he is convinced will and can brook no resistance. The religious life of other religious communities, they exult, is being crushingly destroyed.

And, nearer home, so is that of the Church.

Asia has never quite forgiven the West for its Christian evangelism that voiced its affirmation of its own faith in terms of the death of Asian gods. It will be interesting to see whether Christendom will in the end forgive, or even tolerate, this new evangelism with its comparable proclamation of the death of "the Christian God." This is not to underestimate in either case the power, and even in a certain sense the validity, of the positive faith of the two evangelists. I do stress, however, that there is something radically awry in any faith that can assert itself only through misunderstanding and then denouncing the faith of other men.

What, then, in conclusion, is one to say about the movement, by way of general summing up? Nothing about the future: it has only just begun, and is much too powerful, too quixotic, too explosive for one to predict how it will develop, how men will respond to it. Those of us who sat out the Barthian fashion, preferring sobriety to its inebriating élan, have lived to see its apparent collapse. Yet, even though the modern world is given to extravagant but sporadic fashions, no historian of religion can afford any confidence that a movement such as this, no matter how bizarre, will not catch on. Yet whether it peters out as quickly as it has splashed into prominence, or whether it gives birth to a lasting major new orientation, in any case some generalities seem already clear.

First, the movement does seem to be making faith possible for a goodly number for whom the old symbols had ceased to be eloquent or effective. In Hamilton's poignant words, "In this terrible world, anyone with passionate honesty moves us, and unbelief when it has this passion is more attractive to us than belief when it lacks it" [11]; and he goes on, "We do not glory in our littleness of faith. It saddens and sickens us, and we seek to increase it in company with whoever will listen and speak in the right way" [12]; and again, he speaks of a "pessimism without despair" [13]. Such understatement is disarming and attractive. Actually, it is not unbelief, and I would argue not even littleness of faith, unless measured by purely externalistic standards. It is important to recognize that this movement is one of real faith, of genuine response, of dynamic self-commitment to a vision of the world as it is and as it might be. I leave aside the question of whether it is good or not, and the other question of whether it is Christian or not; but there seems no doubt but that this is a religious movement, dynamic and significant. Some of us had thought that a new religious movement of obviously needed reform that might arise in our day would be intellectually sober, historically sophisticated, and culturally cosmopolitan. This one is none of those things: it is irrational, anti-historical, and parochial. Yet this is the way that many, who could not find faith through the more

---

[11] Hamilton, *op. cit.*, p. 30.   [12] *Ibid.*, p. 31.
[13] *Ibid.*, p. 115.

standard Christian symbols and patterns, are finding it.

It is interesting to speculate on how close or remote the parallel may be between this emergence and that of the movement of the Black Muslims.

Secondly, then, one must note that the movement makes vivid the egregious failure, primarily of other theologians, but of the Church at large, to make intelligible and eloquent the traditional symbols. The alternatives that these men denounce are not so inept or dishonest or obsolete as they make out. Yet the corporations that they represent, while not actually bankrupt—far from it—have in fact not been cashing the cheques that many millions of modern men have tried to draw on them. The treasures in their coffers they have somehow not got into circulation. Anyone more sensitive to the truths and profundities that lie behind the traditional Christian symbols, not merely is disquieted to see how laceratingly these men must flail in order to make their point, but also weeps to recognize how lamentably those charged with explicating the tradition have floundered in their task.

Thirdly, the emergence of this movement makes vivid what some of us had sensed, and even stated, before ever we had heard of the "death of God": namely, that Christianity would seem to be disintegrating as a coherent historical structure. I stress the words "coherent" and "Christianity" and "structure." Personal Christian faith, of course, continues, and will continue. Yet there is so much diversity and clash, so much chaos, in the Christian Church today that the old ideal of a unified or systematic Christian truth has gone. For this, the ecumenical movement is too late. What has happened—Christian "atheists"

carry this forward and make it manifest, but ?
pened already—is that the Christian world has
into that situation where the Hindu has long been: o.
open variety, of optional alternatives. It would seem no
longer possible for anyone to be told, or even to imagine
that he can be told, what it means or should mean,
formally and generically, to be a Christian. He must decide for himself—and only for himself. Authority is gone.
Every man must now decide for himself what he will believe, what symbols he will choose, what myths he will
find significant and will cherish. Every doctrine, as every
image, will be what the Hindus call *istadevata:* "the
chosen god"; or if you like, eclecticism. The "death of
God" movement has, whether we like it or not, and
whether they like it or not, shattered all orthodoxy, and
therefore all heresy, and therefore all alternatives to
eclecticism.

Hindu openness intellectually has been counterbal-
anced socially with a stable, not to say rigid, religio-social
order. Americans counterpoise theological irresponsibil-
ity, or at least individualism, by relying on a social order
called "the American way of life," a virtually absolutized
national structure. Yet one of the matters against which
this revolt has been revolting is the religious/secular
dichotomy that has plagued Western society for long. It
will be a very long time, however, before the profound
difficulties of this situation work themselves out, or perhaps even come to the surface.

The willingness to wreck the Church as a community is,
however, serious.

There is also the point that in berating the Church,

35

they have nothing to offer in its place. They quote the Good Samaritan to prove that a Christian should be up and doing rather than piously attending a Church service; but forget that if it were not for the Church they would never have heard of the Good Samaritan.

The fundamental failure of this movement—but also of its opponents, of those against whom they are revolting—has been a failure to recognize religious symbolism for what it is. To see myth as myth, both one's own and other people's, is the liberation that will allow us, first of all to have faith at all along with our knowledge, in this modern world, and secondly to have a faith without wishing to deride, or to destroy, that of other men. The world has had too much of men who take other people's symbols too seriously, too literally, and because they do not understand them are determined to contemn and to uproot them; and who take their own symbols too seriously, too literally, also, and because they do understand *them*, proclaim them as a final and inescapable (and incompatible) truth.

The word "God" is a symbol; but that to which it refers, is a reality. More accurately, that to which those who have used this word have potentially referred, consciously or unconsciously, is real. It is a reality about which none of us knows enough to be dogmatic or scurrilous; yet about which each of us may, through his own symbols and his own faith, know enough to live—and indeed, to live in a way that is transcendently final.

II IS THE QUR'AN THE WORD OF GOD?

Is the Qur'an the Word of God?

That God speaks, or has spoken, to man has long been a joyous proclamation or quiet assumption of religious faith; more recently, however, it has seemed less clear what such a conviction might mean. I propose that we can illuminate this matter by asking, Is the Qur'an the word of God? This query, I suggest, is worth discussing, is a question that will repay thoughtful consideration for a moment.

By this I do not mean simply that a possible answer to it may be of some significance. Later on we shall spend a certain amount of time formulating some parts of an answer. I shall be presenting for reflection some arguments that may induce perhaps favorable consideration of that particular sort of reply. And I shall be propounding that in any case, any serviceable answer must be rather complex and subtle. Before we reach that stage, however, and whatever one may think of the particular road along which I shall suggest that an answer may be found, the question itself is interesting, and the types of answer that it usually gets. There is reward in pondering some of the matters that such a question involves in the modern world.

First of all, we must observe an arresting fact: that in the past, there have normally been two answers to this question—namely, "yes," and "no." Each of these answers has tended to be clear and straightforward. Some people have given one, some people the other; but whichever it was, it has been given with confident assurance, and even with force. Indeed, for over thirteen centuries now, much of mankind has been divided, quite sharply, into two groups, between whom the boundary has been clear and at times the gulf deep: those that have held that the Qur'an is the word of God, and those who have held that it is not. Now this, I submit, is a remarkably curious situation, once one pauses to reflect on it. Let us elaborate a little on how curious it is.

The question, after all, is not a minor one. If a problem were peripheral to men's serious concerns, then there would be no harm, and little cause for comment, if it went unresolved even for centuries, as this one has. But this question—and others, of course, not unlike it; but this one will suffice to illustrate for us the issues that are involved —this question is manifestly a radically important one. Those who have answered it "yes" have taken the answer passionately. They have been willing to die for it; and what is perhaps more important, if one remarks that people may be stirred to die for many roseate causes, they have been willing to live for it too, to order their lives in accord with it, day after day, year in, year out, generation after generation, patterning their behavior and controlling their choices and selecting their goals, and to persist, firmly but quietly—against both opposition and distraction, against both attack and indifference—in taking it seriously.[1]

[1] Christians are in danger of missing the full force of the Muslim position on this matter, by supposing that the analogy with the Qur'an is

The other group, those whose answer has been "no," have in one sense shown no corresponding passion or fanfare. Yet their persistence has been hardly less steady; and the seriousness of their rejection, not really less. Their conviction has been just as firmly held that the answer is not only "no," but is obviously "no"—so obviously "no" that the matter is not worth bothering about. The West's very indifference to the question is a measure of the profundity of its assurance. Westerners allowed centuries to pass without going around busily asking themselves whether the Qur'an is the word of God, not because they did not have the time or were unconcerned, not because they thought that such issues did not matter (what could matter more?), but because at heart they took for granted that they knew very well what the answer was.

One may guess that this is still true today for many modern men.

Britain at the turn of this century was fairly persuaded that the Indian rope trick was a fake, but it was not totally sure, and was interested in finding out: eager to explore and willing to be convinced. On the Qur'an, on the other hand, the "no" as well as the "yes" group has been certain of its position at a very deep level indeed.

The question, then, is not a minor one. Nor are the groups that have answered it this way or that. It is no small band of eccentrics that holds this book to be God's word; nor is the idea a passing fashion among some

the Bible. Rather, the parallel is to the Christian doctrine that Jesus Christ is the Word of God. Throughout this present discussion, this point should be borne vividly in mind: that the Muslim attitude to the Qur'an is the Christian attitude to Christ.

volatile crowd. Those who have held it are to be numbered in the many hundreds of millions. And as we have
already remarked, it has continued to be held over wide
parts of the world for century after changing century.
Civilizations are not easy to construct, or to sustain; yet
great civilizations have been raised on the basis of this
conviction. Major cultures have sprung from it, winning
the allegiance and inspiring the loyalty and shaping the
dreams and eliciting the poetry of ages proud to bow before its manifest grandeur and, to them, limpid truth. A
thousand years ago the world looked differently from how
it looks today; partly, at that time Europe was an under-
developed area, while the Islamic empires, of whose
splendor a caricature has been preserved for our children in
the Arabian Nights, were the centre of scientific achieve-
ment, of economic might, of military prowess, of artistic
creativity—empires built and manned by those who not
incidentally but centrally said "yes" to the question that
we are considering. On their "yes" they built and held all
their achievements.

Equally impressive, however, have been those who
have said "no." They, too, are not negligible. They, too,
are to be numbered in the hundreds or thousands of millions. They, too, have constructed great civilizations, have
made great cultures dynamic. The outsider distorts his
world if he fails to recognize what has been accomplished
on earth by those inspired by the positive response. The
Muslim distorts *his,* if he fails to appreciate the possibili-
ties evidently open and beckoning to those who say "no."

By this one is not suggesting that the matter is irrelevant. Far from it. To be rejected almost out of hand is any

thesis that religious matters are inconsequential in human history; much modern knowledge can be devoted to championing the opposite. The word of God is or ought to be men's crucial concern. And even the secular historian must reckon much more profoundly than has been his recent wont with man's religiousness and its massive expressions. Islamic history cannot begin to be understood if one fails to see it in its fundamentally Islamic quality. That is trite; but one may go on to say, perhaps a little more provocatively, that European history cannot really be understood either unless its underlying "no" to the Islamic question is taken into account. At certain points this is obvious—Charles Martel at the battle of Poitiers; the Crusades; Lepanto; the siege of Vienna; and so on—but it is true also at many others. The only reason an historian can write the history of Europe without tracing throughout the fact of its resounding or tacit "no" to our question is the simple reason that he takes that "no" so utterly for granted, and presumes so unconsciously that his readers will take it for granted also. Few will dispute the contention that the history not only of the Muslim world but of Christendom would have been seriously different from what it has been, had our question been answered differently, on either side.

The two groups, then, have been numerous; prodigiously numerous. And they have been great; of monumental influence. They have also (and here we approach the heart of our problem) been intelligent. At least, they have included intelligent men; highly intelligent. There have been stupid and petty persons, no doubt, on both sides, and human history would have been different without them. Yet among those who said "yes" to our question, and among those who said "no" to it, there have been men of keen, indeed of superlative, intelligence. Each answer has been sustained by persons brilliant, wise, informed, careful, honest, critical, and sincere. It is sometimes said that people simply accept the religious beliefs with which they are brought up. Yet even if this were true of ninety-nine percent of a community, it would be in a sense quite defensible and hardly worth comment if the other one percent, the leaders whom the followers accept, are independent thinkers. And no historian can argue that it is true of a hundred percent—nor can any preacher, or parent, who know well enough that it is not so easy as such a scoffer suggests, to induce people to accept a truth that you not only have heard but have personally seen. There are blind believers, and there are blind non-believers; but both are logically, and actually, secondary to men whose "yes," and to men whose "no," to our question is reasoned and sincere.

Perhaps what I have been saying will sound platitudinous. We all know that people differ on religious questions, so why the fuss? This brings us to a further matter: that we men have not only given two opposite answers to this question, but we have also come to accept such a fact without disquiet. This is curious. The radical divergence might well make both groups more restless with their own answers than either has often thought it necessary to be. At the very least, there is an intellectual challenge: how is one to rationalize the divergence, to conceptualize it, to interpret it intelligibly? (We leave aside for the moment the theological and the moral impli-

cations; this intellectual problem sufficing us, just now.)
Are our minds to be content to accept lying down the
total divergence, unreconciled, on a major issue?

This acceptance, as a matter of fact, is a little more
complicated than might appear. It does exist, on both
sides. Yet on both sides, it appears on inquiry, there are
certain tendencies toward qualifying it. This is not surprising, since to accept the dichotomy on the intellectual
level, fully, is to set for oneself a quite serious theoretical
problem; and it is easier, certainly more comfortable, to
suppress or evade such problems than to solve them. This
can be done among the negative group, the non-Muslims,
by not recognizing the intelligence to be found on the
other side. If one does not know, or does not appreciate,
this, then it becomes possible to dismiss the other position
as "superstition"—that is, as ideas that are held without
any grounding in reason, and that are not a serious option
for the enlightened.

This stand has, in fact, often been taken, either openly
or surreptitiously, consciously and disdainfully or subtly
and unawares.

On the Muslim side something similar occurs. There
there is also a further, rather subtler rejection. Some Muslims seriously believe that the prophethood of Muhammad
—that is, the belief that the Qur'an comes from God—is
so rational and straightforward as to be self-evident; so that
anyone who rejects it is obtuse or perverse, or both. This
idea underlies a good deal of the bitter Muslim reaction to
the Western academic study of Islamics. Another Muslim
stand questions not the intelligence but the moral integrity
of the "no" group. It supposes that the non-Muslim recog-

nizes the theoretical validity of the Qur'an's being from God but that he nonetheless, for reasons best known to himself (or to God), chooses not to "submit" to it, not to live in accord with its message. I have actually met Muslims who believed this; and who felt that this view paid the Christian the compliment of presuming that he was not so stupid or so spiritually insensitive or so discourteous as to be blind to the Qur'an's authenticity, and accepted him as a strange character who chose not to live up to the vision that had been vouchsafed him. I sometimes wonder if this attitude, conscious or unconscious, on the part of Muslims is perhaps more widespread than one imagines.

However that may be, and however many persons there may be on either side who have not recognized the situation in its true starkness, my own position, quite firmly, is that one must accept, what is empirically the case, both intelligence and sincerity on both sides. A hidden disdain for the other party is a psychologically perhaps satisfying but morally reprehensible and intellectually untenable refuge. Our problem rests on facts, and must be dealt with as such. To the question, Is the Qur'an the word of God? some men, intelligent and sincere, say "yes," and some men, also intelligent, also sincere, say "no."

If we explore this matter somewhat further, an additional refinement becomes necessary—one of great importance. For in actual practice, though the answers have indeed been given, the question has not really been asked. By this I mean that the question, though it logically precedes the answers, historically follows them. It is presupposed, but not formulated. And indeed is not a religious Weltanschauung largely a matter of presuppositions?

The professional task of academic comparative religion-
ists is to intellectualize, if possible, what is going on in the
religious life of the great communities of mankind. Our
business is precisely to bring into the open in theoretical
formulation the positions that men of faith inwardly take,
and particularly to bring into the open the questions to
which their religious positions are the answer. In most
cases, of course, this is a very much more exacting and
subtle affair than in the present one. Sometimes it takes
years of patient exploration, and great depths of sensitive
understanding, to discern what those questions are. Yet
even in the present case, where the question is quite
straightforward and obvious, nonetheless in practice it
has hardly ever been asked. This fact too can be illuminat-
ing.

In the Muslim world, you will not find, or would not
have found for centuries gone by, a lecture announced for
theologians carrying as its title the question with which
we have begun this chapter. Nor do I know of any book in
the Muslim world with this title. Muslims do not publicly
ask, Is the Qur'an the word of God. There are many
books, and no doubt there have been many lectures, in
which the answer (the affirmative answer) has been
given. But there are not books, and have not been lectures, in which the question was asked; precisely because
the answer was given, was known, was accepted. Perhaps
it was not firmly accepted, and had to be argued, or
explained, buttressed or confirmed. Hence the books.
Hence the long debates among the theological schools,
the long explanations and discriminations, the interpretations of meaning, the ferreting out of subtleties, the long

47

history of theological discussion and conflict. Yet the whole discussion and debate, with all its ramifications, comes under the heading of answer, not under the heading of question.

Similarly in the West. Without looking into the matter, one may guess that it was probably novel that a lecture by a Christian minister in a Christian theological setting should bear the title, "Is the Qur'an the word of God?" as happened when the draft of these chapters was first given as the Taylor Lectures at Yale Divinity School. Again, the reason is the same: the question has not been asked, because the answer has been constant. One may suppose that anyone who undertook to go through previous Taylor Lecture series at Yale would find the answer "no" to our question given many, many times; and certainly in other theological seminaries, and other activities of Christendom over the centuries, the answer "no" has been reiterated endlessly. We said at the beginning that we would ask that this question be considered seriously; in asking this, it appears, one is asking not only something perhaps novel, but even something searching, something radical. Indeed, one of the profound movements of our time, of which the leaders of the Church are restlessly and uncomfortably aware, is that the Church, inchoately but disturbingly, is beginning to ask this kind of question, not rhetorically, but genuinely. It is beginning to ask it because it is beginning to feel, inchoately but disturbingly, that the long-standing answers may not be adequate; or at least that they are not self-evident.

The Muslim world, also, is moving into what may possibly become a profound crisis, too; in that it also is just beginning to ask this question, instead of being content only with answering it. Young people in Lahore and Cairo, labor leaders in Jakarta and Istanbul, are beginning to ask their religious thinkers, and beginning to ask themselves, "Is the Qur'an the word of God?" Answering this question has been the business of the Muslim world for over thirteen centuries. Asking it is a different matter altogether, haunting and ominous.

In fact, the question, Is the Qur'an the word of God? insofar as it is a genuine question, is a threat—both to Christian and to Muslim theology, simultaneously and for the same reason.

A Christian theologian who asks it would be probably at least a heretic, if that category of thought were still in use. A Muslim who asked it publicly today might quite possibly be killed.

Before we explore this explosive matter, however—the dynamics of modernity; the transformation through which we are living, or on which at least we are embarked— there remains one major point about the past positions, the answers. Each side has tended to think of the other as prejudiced. If one removes the pejorative flavor of that accusation, there is a certain validity on both sides, in the technical sense that each position is in fact a "pre-judgement," a coming to the problem with one's mind already made up. Muslims do not read the Qur'an and conclude that it is divine; rather, they believe that it is divine, and then they read it. This makes a great deal of difference, and I urge upon Christian or secular students of the Qur'an that if they wish to understand it as a religious document, they must approach it in this spirit. If an

outsider picks up the book and goes through it even asking himself, What is there here that has led Muslims to
suppose this from God? he will miss the reverberating impact. If, on the other hand, he picks up the book and asks
himself, What would these sentences convey to me if I
believed them to be God's word? then he can much more
effectively understand what has been happening these
many centuries in the Muslim world.

It is not only Christian theologians or missionaries,
however, whose answer has been a taken-for-granted "no."
The Western academic scholar, too, has not studied the
Qur'an, asking himself whether this be divine or human.
He has presumed before he started that it was human,
and he has studied it in that light. Some of the more sensitive outside scholars have remembered, as they studied,
that *Muslims* believe this to be God's word; others have
done not even that, one would judge from their writing;
but virtually none of them, quite manifestly, has ever
asked himself, Is God speaking to *me* in these words? I
said just now that I doubt whether Christian ministers
have in the past lectured to ministers under a title, "Is the
Qur'an the Word of God?" I am quite confident that no
academic scholar in the West has ever lectured on this
theme. For one may be sure that the question has never
occurred to him to be needing asking. If you scrutinize
the scholarly studies of such Western students of the
Qur'an as Jeffery, Richard Bell, Blachère, von Kremer,
and the others, you will realize that such a possibility
never once entered their minds. They did not conclude
that the Qur'an is the word of Muhammad; they started
with that view, which was never for a moment chal-

lenged. One of them, even, has formulated it in so many words (unwittingly, of course: he was simply dealing with the question of whether the text now available is historically reliable). He wrote: "We hold the Qur'an to be as veritably the word of Muhammad, as Muslims hold it to be the word of God."

Both the "yes" and the "no" positions, then, are preconvictions.

Secondly—and this is major—both positions work. Each has found a pragmatic justification. Those who adopt either position, and follow it through consistently, find their reward. Perhaps there is in the end no more cogent argument for any religious position, Christian or other, than that those who adopt it find that it authenticates itself. "Our fathers have lived by it over the centuries, and it has proven itself to them; we have tried it ourselves, and we find that it is true." Those who have held the Qur'an to be the word of God have, by holding this, found that God does in fact speak to them through it. They have ordered their lives in accord with it, and have found that that pattern rewards them by bringing them into the divine presence. The Book promises to those who submit to its letter and spirit, guidance and boldness and inner peace and endurance in this world, and felicity in the next. We have no evidence on affairs in the next world, but so far as this world is concerned the promise, to those who believe, has in fact been redeemed. Islamic history, and the godliness of my personal Muslim friends, corroborate the Muslim's affirmative answer.

Equally striking, the outsider's negative answer is also self-authenticating. Western scholars, such as those that I have mentioned, and many others, approach the Qur'an quite heedless of a possibility that it might be God's word; persuaded that its source was mundane, they look for that source in the psychology of Muhammad, in the environment in which he lived, in the historical tradition that he inherited, in the socio-economic-cultural milieu of his hearers. They look for it, and they find it. They find it, because quite evidently it is there. Muslims may protest all they like that such scholars are dishonest; the fact is that they are human, and like all scholars they may and do make mistakes, and like all scholars they admit it, and yet essentially they have been motivated by intellectual integrity, by scientific method, by disinterested, disciplined inquiry. Where their hypotheses have failed to explain the facts, they have changed the hypotheses, or at least the next generation has. Not only does the method work; it has proven enormously fruitful. Western scholarship on the Qur'an has uncovered a mass of material otherwise quite lost; has reconstructed an historical picture, has traced developments, has established interpretations, that are unassailable.

Those who hold the Qur'an to be the word of God, have found that this conviction leads them to a knowledge of God. Those who hold it to be the word of Muhammad, have found that this conviction leads them to a knowledge of Muhammad. Each regards the other as blind. From what I have said, you will perhaps discern that in this matter I feel that in fact each is right.

So much for the past. In a schematically simplified way I have delineated the situation that has arisen over the centuries as men have adopted one or the other of two essentially dogmatic and contradictory answers to our question. I have hinted that at the present time in this matter, as in every other in which man is involved, change is beginning to be discernible. And for the future, I am prepared to speculate that something quite new in this realm both will and should develop—new not only in content but in form.

As we have remarked, in the past there have been essentially two answers to our question; namely, "yes," and "no." These answers have been both personal, and social; but even in the personal case, they have tended to be not individualist, but in groups. A whole community has given one answer, and a whole community the other. The two groups have then lived in isolation from each other, in basic ignorance of each other. And such contact as there has been between the two has more often than not been conflict—suppressed, in rivalry and disdain, or overt, in war. From now on, one may devoutly hope that the violence at least, and presently the conflict and even the disdain, have been or may be left behind. And the isolation and ignorance are in process of departing, from both sides. Civilizations in the past lived insouciant of each other; this is no longer so, and clearly, for the future, we shall be living in "one world." We have become aware of each other, quite vividly; and are gradually becoming aware of each other at a cultural and even a theological level, so that our lives from now on are to be lived in a global society in which all of us are intermingling participants.

So far as our particular problem goes, this means that the days are surely over when we can be content with a situation in which some of us, either glibly or emphatically, give one, and others of us give another, of two stridently different answers to what has appeared to both of us to be a relatively straightforward, and certainly an important, question. At least, I for one am simply intellectually restless at so conspicuously irrational a dichotomy. As an intellectual, I feel challenged by the theoretical incoherence; I feel driven to strive for an answer that, if it has not yet attained universal validity, will at least have transcended the evident limitations of the dichotomized past.

Of course, another possible reaction to the discomfort of an intolerable contradiction is not on the intellectual level but on a practical: to seek a solution not by finding a new answer intellectually that will do justice to the facts of the present polarity, but by striving to create a new situation, in which the dichotomy will have been replaced by a uniformity. On the Muslim side, this moral response takes the form of missions. The Islamic has been one of the three or four great missionary movements on our planet. Throughout Islamic history there have been those unwilling to accept a world divided into those that answered "yes" and those that answered "no," who therefore set out to convert the others, so that all would say "yes." In the other direction, a counterpart is a possible debunking mission, aimed at discouraging any "yes" answer. We may note that in the past this debunking has been common both to Western secularists and to Christians, the latter having taken for granted that to affirm Christ as the word of God "of course" involves saying "no" to the Qur'an's being the word of God too.

We shall return to this point later; at the moment I would simply remark that it does not seem likely that the intellectual problem will be solved for us in this missionary way—in either direction—by changing the status quo so radically that the question will no longer arise.

I do not know how many will share my sense of an intellectualist imperative to construct a theoretical answer more comprehensive, coherent, and unifying than the traditional ones. Quite apart from that, anyway, there are certain contemporary historical considerations to which one must attend. These indicate that—whether we like it or not—new types of answer, new analyses of the question, are in fact being engendered. These considerations are directly related to the point that we have just made: that the isolation of the two groups is giving way to an intermingling, and the ignorance of each for the other is giving way to awareness.

I have argued that each of the two groups' answers does, in fact, work. This is true on its own premises, and within the confines of its own group. One may rephrase the situation more accurately, by saying that each *has* worked, for its own group, so long as the isolation of that group from the other has been maintained. Now that that isolation is disappearing, however, both the pragmatic and the theoretical justification of each answer is proving inadequate.

Let us take the "no" answer first, as it has been worked out carefully by Western orientalist scholarship. That answer, we have said, has shown itself capable of accounting for all the facts about the Qur'an—except the facts of the religious life of the Muslim community, the life that has developed since, among those who have said "yes" to our question. Western scholarship on the Qur'an has taken the Qur'an as a seventh-century-Arabian document; and, as such, has analysed and explained it roundly. It has not much considered it, however, and has not much explained it, as an eighth- and a twelfth- and a twentieth-century document, as a continuingly contemporary and timeless book on which the faith of men of faith has been continuingly fed. It has studied it as a literary document, and has brilliantly understood it as a literary document. It has done little to understand it, or even to try to understand it, as a religious document: living, life-giving, the point at which the eternal not only is thought to, but for a devout Muslim actually does, break through into time, lifting him out of his historical environment and introducing him, not only in theory but in exuberant practice, to transcendence. How the Qur'an came to be what it is, is one question, to which the Western sceptic has addressed himself. How the Qur'an came to do what it has done, for believing Muslims across the centuries since, is another: the actual life-giving source of the religious life of the continuing community.

As this latter is becoming more known, as contact has grown with living Muslims as men of faith, as knowledge and insight have increased not only into the outward facts of Islamic history but into the inward life of those who have lived within that history as servants of a living and speaking God; so the awareness has come that the traditional Western answer explains only some of the phenomena. It is true insofar as it goes, but it has become increasingly evident that it does not go far enough.

We said above that scientific inquiry stands ever ready to modify its hypothesis; and as a matter of fact, the non-Muslim West has just begun to soften, even to withdraw, its "no." In a recent article, the professor of Arabic at Harvard, Sir Hamilton Gibb, doyen of Western Islamicists, explicitly states in passing: "For myself, I unhesitatingly accept the term 'Revelation' (in Arabic *tanzīl*, "sending down" or *waḥy*, "inner communication") as the description of Muḥammad's personal experience, although Islam, like the other monotheistic religions, is faced with the necessity of reinterpreting the no longer tenable mediaeval concepts of 'revelation'." [2]

Similarly, a Christian theologian like Kenneth Cragg, leading theorist of Protestant missions to Muslims, no longer responds to the Qur'an by rejecting it theologically.[3] And it seems clear that the next generation of scholars, without accepting the traditional Muslim answer, will go beyond the traditional non-Muslim one. What answer they will give is not yet evident, not even to them; so that it is not too fanciful to suggest that the non-Muslim observer of Islam is for the first time engaged in asking the question that we are discussing. He is in the midst of a search, and will soon be increasingly self-consciously in the midst of a search, for a new type of answer: neither a simple "yes" nor a simple "no" but some *tertium quid*, more subtle, more complex, tentative, yet to be hammered out.

[2] Hamilton A. R. Gibb, "Pre-Islamic Monotheism in Arabia," *Harvard Theological Review*, 55: 269 (1962).

[3] See, for instance, his *The Call of the Minaret* (New York, 1956) and *Sandals at the Mosque* (New York, 1959).

Similar considerations pertain for the Muslim world, for the group that has traditionally answered a straight-forward "yes." This answer, too, has worked; it has proved richly rewarding, fruitful, creative. It has justified itself. Yet it too has worked within its own premises, and has justified itself within a community isolated in large part from others. Just as the "no" answer has served satisfactorily to explain the Qur'an itself, but not to explain the facts to which the "yes" answer has given rise, so in reverse the "yes" answer of the Muslims has served to cope with the Qur'an itself, but it does not cope with the facts to which the "no" answer has given rise. The Muslims' affirmative answer, or the elaborations of it that the community has developed, have been able to handle the matters that have arisen within the community. But in our day it has been proving itself incapable of handling the new historical data that Western scholarship on the Qur'an, for example, has been not only uncovering but making available also to Muslims. The knowledge, the reconstructions, that sceptical historical criticism from abroad has purveyed, makes the traditional "yes" answer, in its traditional form, inadequate.

Until now, the situation has been rather desperately complicated by political overtones: Western scholarship has been resisted, or decried, by Muslims as a tool of Western imperialism, as something deliberately calculated to undermine Muslims' faith; malicious, hopefully irrelevant. Yet even those who do not feel that Western imperialism is a horse too dead to be worth flogging any more, are not immune from a new emergence. For this non-Muslim scholarship is being taken up these days not only by the infidel West, but by Hindus in India and

Buddhists in Japan, and to some degree even by the new generation of Muslims themselves. Isolationism is going; in principle, it is gone. Like the rest of us, Muslims from now on are going to have to live their lives, even their religious lives, as participant members of a world community.

The historical facts that give sense to the proposition that the Qur'an is a mundane product, can no more be gainsaid by Muslims than can, by outside observers, the religious facts that give sense to the proposition that it is a divine word, a power of God unto salvation for those that believe.

One symbol of the end of isolation are the new collaborative academic centers that are being set up, in which Western scholars and Muslims work together toward understanding, so that every remark about Islam by a Westerner is consciously made in the presence of Muslims, and every remark about Islam by a Muslim is explicitly made in the presence of those who cannot give a simple "yes" to our question.

And although much of the Muslim world is on the defensive against what seems to it the attacks and threats of outside theories, nonetheless the best minds and most honest spirits in that community are themselves sincerely searching for a new answer to our question, one that will do equal justice to the transcendent element in their tradition, and yet will at the same time be meaningful and persuasive to those whose horizon is global and whose historical understanding is realistic. As a modernist Pakistani has shown in a revealing study [4], the answers of acute

[4] F. Rahman, *Prophecy in Islam* (London and New York, 1958).

minds in classical Islamic terms themselves to our question were not so simplicist as more recent conceptions would suggest. A Muslim friend told me once that his wife was startled to learn (from him) that the Qur'an did not "come down" to Muhammad from heaven as a bound volume; another Muslim friend once told me that, for him, the Qur'an was the word of God to Muhammad just as *The Messiah* was "revealed" to Handel who said of it that the heavens were opened to him and he heard this music and wrote it down.

In other words, the Muslim world also is beginning to be in search of an answer to our question more subtle, more realistic, more historical, more complex than the traditional "yes or no."

Significant in this new situation, where both traditional groups are setting out in search of a larger answer, is the fantastically potential novelty that, in the process, both groups are beginning to deliberate on each other's books.

Perhaps because I believe seriously in the unity of knowledge, and believe seriously in the unity of mankind, I rather imagine that the only answer to our question that will satisfy the non-Muslim and the only answer that will satisfy the Muslim will in coming years be identical. I am not unaware that this is a radical position, crucial for Christian theology and also for Islamic. That it is radical does not disturb me, since I am deeply persuaded that in the twentieth and twenty-first centuries the religious history of mankind will be taking a major new turn. We shall not go here into that rather elaborate and problematic matter. Yet that Christian theology must, and I think will, ponder this question, and hammer out some answer for itself, is both an illustration and a measure of the newness of not only Christian life, but of Muslim life as well. I cannot see how in principle any answer to our question can be truly adequate for a Christian unless it were also and simultaneously truly adequate for a Muslim; and yet if that be true, how profoundly novel the religious history of both our groups has become!

I do not mean that Christians and Muslims will cease to be different; but I do suggest that intellectually their understandings must converge, even if morally they choose to respond differently. Reactions to the universe, the existential religious response, may presumably continue to be a personal or group adventure. Theory, on the other hand, it is the business of those of us who are intellectuals to universalize.

I have elsewhere elaborated the thesis that the task of comparative religion is that of constructing statements that will be true in more than one tradition simultaneously. Even if one does not wish to follow me here, nonetheless the minimum fact that from now on Christian theologians will be professionally at work on a central issue of Islamic theology (and perhaps presently also vice-versa) will make it not only true, but vivid, that a new age in man's religious development is being ushered in.

(In passing, one may also let drop the suggestion that the dawning of this new age is relevant to the otherwise vexed question of the future of Christian missions. Also, of Muslim missions.)

We live, then, in a world where for all men a question such as that with which we began is becoming an open question, to which the answer is not known but has to be discovered; and where the question itself is no longer simple, but has to be understood.[5] One may at a minimum suggest that we do not yet know fully all the ways in which God has spoken, and speaks, to man.

[5] It is perhaps unnecessary to add (I hope the point has been manifestly implicit throughout) that this whole discussion may presumably be transposed, whether on to parallel Hindu or Buddhist issues, or back into internal Christian terms. A consideration of the Western/Muslim divergence over the Qur'an is applicable at least in principle to a secular/Christian divergence over Christian positions. To suppose that there is, or even ideally should be, a generic 'yes' or 'no' answer to such questions as whether Christ is the Word, or the Son, the incarnate revelation, of God, must surely be superseded. The question remains as important, as destiny-determining, as ever it was; but the answer is not so simple, is no longer impersonal.

III CAN RELIGIONS BE TRUE OR FALSE?

Can Religions be True or False?

Are religions true or false? is a question that might, at first blush, appear rhetorical. In grammar, a rhetorical question is one that "does not expect an answer": the question itself carries the punch, and conveys the meaning. To answer it would be otiose, an anticlimax. For the answer is supposed to be obvious, because generally agreed; while the question is what makes the point. On more careful reflection, one recognizes that in this particular case the matter is not quite so. As in the instance of our preceding chapter, so here it is rather the answers that have been rhetorical, as it were; making some emphatic point, while the question itself goes unexpressed. In this present realm, answers have been far from generally agreed: men have made striking points by affirming this or that, in vigorous clash one with another, while all have seemed to take for granted the legitimacy and innocence of the questions. "All religions are true," someone has said, feeling that he has said something wise and weighty. "All religions are false," opines another, confident that the dictum is dramatic and pungent. "This religion is true, others false," is a third conviction, of one who expects that some people may disagree perhaps with his verdict, but not that they will fail themselves to be asking the question to which this is his, however particular, answer.

A whole series of answers are synthesized in the cynic's witticism: "All religions are, to the believer, equally true; to the philosopher, equally false; and to the politician, equally useful." If we can somehow turn the flank of that remark's cynicism, and the others' divergence, we may attain some illumination.

There is no general agreement among men, and perhaps no prospect of agreement, as to which religions are true, or false, or whether they are; but *that* they are true or false would seem a notion that, you may agree, is widespread.[1]

That a notion is widespread is not, however, an argument against scrutinizing it; and this one, I suggest, will repay consideration. I ask you to reflect with me for a moment not on the answers but on the question—or at least on some considerations that bear on any attempt to characterize religious life, our own or other men's, in these particular terms.

I have recently published a book to which, whatever other merits or defects it may have, one will perhaps concede at least the virtue of boldness when I say, to oversimplify the argument drastically, that it contends that there are no such things on earth as religions—on earth, or in heaven either, for that matter.[2] If there are no reli-

---

[1] A certain school in philosophy has suggested that *religious statements* may be neither true nor false; but meaningless, rather. This is quite a different matter. We shall shift consideration to that level later on in this chapter.

[2] *The Meaning and End of Religion: a New Approach to the Religious Traditions of Mankind* (New York, 1963).

gions, then clearly they cannot be true or false, and the matter is ended.

That, however, is overly cute, you may feel, or evasive; and I am assuredly not seeking evasion. I remark that this description of the book is oversimplified; and when I say that there are no religions, I am modern enough to mean, of course, that the phenomena usually conceptualized so are better—more truly—conceived under other categories. Indeed my endeavor to construct an alternative theoretical framework for interpreting to ourselves the religious history of man, is *inter alia* an endeavor to deal more adequately with precisely this question of religious truth and falsity—a question of which I certainly do not belittle the importance, and quarrel only with the form. I will not repeat here, however, the elaborate argument propounded in that study. Let us leave it aside, and approach the matter from a different angle: attempting to show some problems that indicate difficulties in the more accustomed viewpoint. If one were not to abandon the concept "religions," what would be involved in thinking of them as true or false?

Let me repeat: I seek no evasion. Religious truth is utterly crucial; is the paramount and inescapable issue, before which all other religious matters, however mighty, must bow. It is final. The great question, however, is, where does it lie—and the immediate question, does it lie in the religions. I am suggesting that it does not (that it lies elsewhere; namely, in persons).

I personally advocate our dropping the term "Christianity"; but if it is used, then I would argue with vigor that it is dangerous and impious to suppose that Christianity is true, as an abstract system, something "out there" impersonally subsisting, with which we can take some comfort therefore in being linked—its effortless truth justifying us, and giving us status. Christianity, I would suggest, is not true absolutely, impersonally, statically; rather, it can *become* true, if and as you or I appropriate it to ourselves and interiorize it, insofar as we live it out from day to day. It becomes true as we take it off the shelf and personalize it, in dynamic actual existence.

The trouble is, of course, and this is desperately significant, that also it may become false. I can falsify Christianity. And the terrifying point is that I do falsify it. The truth of some abstract system labeled "Christianity" is neither here nor there to me so long as it remains alien to my personal existence. Religious life is no theoretical pattern or intellectualist abstraction, independent of personal involvement and of day-to-day moral life. Therefore to say that Christianity is true is to say nothing significant; the only question that concerns either God, or me, or my neighbor is whether *my* Christianity is true, and whether yours is. And to that question, a truly cosmic one, in my case the only valid answer is a sorrowful "not very." By my Christianity I mean my actual, living Christianity, my Christianness, the specific religion of my personal life. If I escape, by grace, the situation where that Christianity of mine can be described only as false, even so the best to which I can rise, alas, is that it is not so true as it ought to be. Anything less realistic is glib.

Furthermore, my Christianity may be more true this morning than it was yesterday afternoon. It may collapse altogether in some crisis tomorrow morning; whereas one

day ten years ago in some particular encounter its truth
may have risen for a moment to serious significance.
Again, one man's Christianity may be (must be) more
false than another's. Your Christianity may be truer than
the Christianity of your next-door neighbor. I know two
Christians of whom the religion of one is more true than
the religion of the other.

This kind of point is none too radical, perhaps, though
it is important, and should guide our thinking. Its significance appears more teasingly, however, if one considers
the faith of men of another community. I also have two
Muslim friends, of whom the religion of one is more true
than the religion of the other.

Many Muslims have tended to affirm that Islam is the
true religion; and some among them, neglecting to heed
the warning that even so it requires to *become* true in
their personal, concrete life, have lulled themselves into
complacency by passively applauding its abstract truth
while doing nothing about it, or by basking in the assurance that this true religion contains within itself the ideal
solution to all men's problems, while those problems in
fact go unsolved, partly because *their* personal Islam is
not a living, dynamic, *true* faith. It matters less whether
Islam as an impersonal and ineffective entity, in essence
but not in existence, is true or not—and indeed, it means
less—than whether the actual Islam of Muslim X, and
Muslim Y, and Muslim Z is true religion, or how far it is;
how far it was true yesterday morning, again, and how far
it is true this evening. This last matters to the rest of us,
and matters to the Muslims concerned. That it alone matters even to God is suggested perhaps in that according to

the Qur'an the Day of Judgement will see not abstract religious entities on trial before the throne, but men and women.

"True" and "false" here mean not only true to some Islamic prototype, or false to it; they mean, or can mean, true religion, true to the prototype of what religion ought to be. This point can become clear, and fruitful, when one considers the hypothetical and perhaps extreme case where we may postulate some outsider—for example, perhaps some reader of these pages—who may believe that Islam is a false religion, just as some Muslims believe that Hinduism is a false religion. Such a man has still to ask himself whether—or better, how far—the religiousness of a particular Muslim or a particular Hindu on a particular October afternoon in a specific context was true. To say that Christianity is true does not tell us anything about how false the Christianity of Mr. Q may have been last week when he was putting across some real-estate deal. To say that Islam or Hinduism is false does not tell us anything about how true the religion of a particular Jordanian peasant or Indian diplomat may have been as he walked up the road from Jericho one day last spring and helped a man lying in distress by the roadside whom a Christian priest and a Canadian tourist passing that way had been too busy to bother with.

Or let us take a more theological example. A devout person, whose sense of the presence of God is both vivid and sincere, and of his own unworthiness as he bows in that presence, may plead for God's mercy, and humbly know the quiet transport of its assurance because of his personal and living faith that God is indeed merciful. At

that moment the truth of that man's religiousness is perhaps a different matter from the question of the earthly
path by which he arrived at his awareness and his faith,
or of the community of which he is a member. The truth
of his religion in its actual, living quality—the private,
personal religion that is really and significantly *his*—is a
different question from, and again I would say a more interesting question to God Himself, as well as to you and
me, than, any question of the truth or otherwise of "his
religion" in the abstract, formal, systematic sense of the
religion of his historical community generally. We talk
blandly of the religion to which he belongs; ought we not
rather to concern ourselves with the religion that belongs
to him? God is interested in persons, not in types.

The fundamental point is this. The religion of one
Christian may be more true, or more false, at a given
moment than at another moment, or than the religion of
another Christian. This must be understood. The religion
of one Muslim may be more true, or more false, at a given
moment than at another moment, or than the religion of
another Muslim. This must be conceded, must be grasped,
in all its terrifying and its life-giving quality.

Once it is grasped, a vital issue follows. The question of
serious significance then becomes: may the religion of a
particular Christian be more true, and may it be more
false, than the religion of a particular Muslim?

This is a genuine question. The answer is not obvious.
Some Christians and some Muslims (and some atheists?)
will agree together in answering it "yes"; other Christians
and other Muslims (and other atheists) will agree together in answering it "no." At the moment I will not an-

swer it; but only suggest that it is a more searching and more important question than the traditional query as to whether Christianity or Islam is true in general; more difficult to answer, but more rewarding. Whichever way you answer it, serious implications emerge.

One interesting point is that those Christians and those Muslims who reject the "yes" answer as relativist, hold their views independently of any study of history. (Traditionally, most religious views have been held independently of any study of other men's history.) Their conclusion is arrived at, and sustained, not on the basis of observation but on that of prior theory. So far as observation is concerned, I think it would be quite impossible to challenge the following contention: that if the terms "true" and "false" here have any meaning or relevance, then the concrete, personal religious life of a particular Christian may be more true, and it may be more false, than that of a particular Muslim. Now this does not in itself finally prove anything; not all religious questions are answered by empirical observation. The theory might be true, and the historical view false. All that I would plead for the moment is that the theory be conscious and adequate. I am sure that it is not impossible to formulate a theology that will rationalize the position, either for the Christian or, *mutatis mutandis,* for the Muslim (I could proffer one myself, for either group). I would simply plead that it must address itself to this question; and would insist that this is not disposed of by any glib conviction that any one religion in general is true or false. Thinking must be more strenuous than that, more realistic and aware, if it is to serve a useful purpose today.

By taking the Christian and Islamic instances as illustrations, we have illuminated perhaps one facet of our problem, but failed to illuminate another, to which we should now turn. I have urged the personalist quality of religious life as of ultimate significance, over against abstract system. This, whether valid or not, is relevant in these two cases where an abstract system has come to be formulated. This has come about quite recently, by the way, as I have elsewhere historically documented. It is a surprisingly modern aberration for anyone to think that Christianity is true or that Islam is—since the Enlightenment, basically, when Europe began to postulate religions as intellectualist systems, patterns of doctrine, so that they could for the first time be labeled "Christianity" and "Buddhism," and could be called true and false. Earlier this was not so. No classical Christian theologian, I have discovered, ever said that Christianity is true. When the Protestant Reformer Zwingli, for instance, wrote a treatise *De Vera et Falsa Religione,* he was talking, as he says in his opening sentence, about the true and false religion of Christians. I translate his title as "On Genuine and Spurious Piety." As one would expect from a Reformer, he knew very well that Christians could falsify their religion. He was not at all concerned to think that other religions are false, ideally; rather, he was concerned that his own (and ours?) might be, actually—which is healthier and more realistic.[3]

Be that as it may, the Christian and the Islamic cases have lent themselves to the recent systematizing process, to what I call "reification." This situation is not universal.

[3] Cf. *The Meaning and End of Religion,* Chaps. 2 and 3.

The Hindu tradition is notoriously less structured and integrated than our Christian one, or than the Muslim's; and this is not by chance, but is a matter of principle with them. Many Hindus reject deliberately, and thoughtfully, a notion that there is a given pattern of religious truth or of salvation, independent of the persons who may perceive it or move toward it. Hindus are so cheerfully diverse, so insistent that religious ways are many, that only vast and distorting oversimplification could predicate that their diversity and their ways is (I say "ways is" to enforce my point) false or true. No Hindu has said anything that some other Hindu has not contradicted; so that people who go in for generalizations are put on their mettle in that land. In historical fact, Christian and Muslim developments have been actually diverse, also. We, however, deplore our divisions and have tended to feel that ideally at least there is one Christian, one Islamic, truth; whereas Hindus delight in multiformity, and tend to hold that personal religious truth has not become sharp if it does not prick the bubble of generalization.

The Buddhist case is somewhat similar, somewhat different. The Buddhist tradition also has developed a vast richness of diversity, especially in its Mahayana evolution; a diversity of which it is not ashamed. One small way of calling attention to the historical variety, might be to assert, what I have no hesitation in putting forward, that no man in one lifetime of study could possibly become sufficiently well informed on the history of either the Buddhist or the Hindu communities to be able to say that Buddhism or Hinduism is true, or alternatively is false, and know what he was saying.

Of a tradition like our Christian one, which feels that its position can in some sense be summed up in a single formula, such as the Apostles' Creed, or in a corpus such at the official teaching of the Church, and which feels that too great richness of diversity may be discounted by being sloughed off as in some sense "heresy"—of such a tradition one may dream perhaps of postulating predicates. Of traditions like the Hindu and the Buddhist, on the other hand, the idea of predicating anything at all is modern, Western, and unfeasible.

That it is modern and Western I have been able to document historically, objectively. That it is unfeasible is my own contention, which I am submitting for consideration. (One would have to know a good deal to refute it.)

One more implication of this evolutionary exuberance, this historical creativity if one may call it that, is of perhaps increasing relevance; namely, the future. With traditions that are manifestly and self-consciously in flux, that do not hold the view that final religious truth has been given in the past, the situation to date might in principle be assessed—yet the future is open. Who can possibly know what Hindu faith will become tomorrow? Who knows what new *yana* the Buddhists may decide, or may be inspired or persuaded, to launch? To say that a religion of *this* type is true, or is false, must at the very most give way to a judgement that it has been true, or has been false, till now. I personally believe that if one is going to talk of religions at all, then one must recognize that every religion is new every morning. Some might wish to exclude their own reified system from this, at the price of depersonalizing it; but no one can exclude the Hindu and

Buddhist traditions. One might argue, certainly, that no matter what happens to these, no matter how they develop, they will still be illegitimate if they do not include Christ (or, the Qur'an). Yet how can one know that they will not include Christ, or the Qur'an (or both)—or, if they do, in what form?

Rather than what is in general, religious truth is, I suggest, a matter of what is in actuality; and therefore, also, of what has been, and what will be. The future religious history of mankind is open.

Even those who like to think that religions have been false in the past, should hope that they will become true in the future.

If missionary policy planners have an ear to hear, let them hear.

There remains still another facet to all this; one that may be illustrated by these world traditions, but also by much simpler ones, such as that of the Andaman Islands or some African bushmen. Every human community on earth has a tradition of practices and institutions and customs that Westerners may call its religion; yet what would be meant by affirming those practices and institutions and customs to be true, or to be false, is not quite clear. A tribe meets to celebrate its harvest according to an ancestral custom; or performs a ritual dance, or solemnizes a marriage, or sanctifies a death. Is this behavior *true*, or false? Or perhaps one might say, is this *behavior* true or false?

Since the Enlightenment, with its rationalist and intellectualizing emphases, we Westerners have laid much stress on doctrine, and have tended to equate religion with belief; and ever since the Greek impact on the Church we Christians have in fact given a highly important role to theology. Not all religious groups, however, share these particular orientations with us. There is really very little justification for the habit that we have built up of going about asking, with regard to various religious groups, What do they believe? as though this were a central, or at least a legitimate, question. What do they do? What do they feel? What do they hope, and fear? How are they related to each other and to God? These and many others are much more significant matters. Most tribes do have a mythology to go with their rites and their involvements; but in what sense they "believe" their mythology is not altogether clear. (Apart from that, we Christians have decided that the truth of Christianity does not stand or fall with the Garden of Eden; but I let that pass.) You may say that the religious life of a given tribe is beautiful or ugly, edifying or wicked, rational or grotesque, poetic or prosaic, helpful or obstructive, cohesive or disruptive; you may say that it is the opiate of people, or the form of social progress; the channel through which they know God insofar as they do know Him, or a totally human contrivance with no relevance to the divine; you may say that it is pleasing to God, or displeasing. But what would you mean by saying that it is true or false?

We were speaking just now of "Hinduism" and "Buddhism" (I stress the quotation marks around those words —it will be remembered that I myself no longer use these terms, nor consider them legitimate). I said that the historical proliferation of those traditions has been so abundant that no one can apprehend them. I was aware that

77

the argument was left incomplete; for I could understand what might prompt a Christian or a Muslim of a certain type to reply, "I do not know what Hinduism or Buddhism is, but whatever it is I know that it is false." I could understand this; and though I do not like it, I should not wish, at this moment, to challenge the theological premises on which the conclusion rests. (I have done so elsewhere.) My concern at this point is to question only the predicate. If one does not know what a thing is, even if one believes —let us say, because of one's interpretation of revelation —that God rejects it, or rejects those persons who participate in it, how can one possibly know that the term "false" is applicable to it? It might perhaps be deemed nonsaving. But our question, you will remember, is: Can religions be true or false?

Certainly, as will be seen in our next chapter, I would not rule out a Platonic truth of things, in favor of an Aristotelian truth of propositions. Yet I would plead for seriousness here; with an awareness both as to the kind of truth and falsity involved, and as to the kind of thing to which they are being attributed.

The religious traditions of mankind are facts, not theories. Some have theories that go with them, though not all; and even those that do, such as the Christian, are a trifle less sure today than yesterday that the theories are primary or ultimate (or exhaustive). What are called "the religions" exist. They are simply there, like Mount Everest. Like Mount Everest, you may like them, or you may not; you may decide to climb them, or you may not; you may feel that you can trust them to bear your weight or not, or the weight of those who, unlike you, have pitched their tents on their slopes. Yet whatever your attitude to them, they are more like Mount Everest than they are like a proposition in science. The latter may be true or false, but historical facts and social institutions are existent actualities.

Of course, this analogy is not close, for they are all in motion. They are in some ways more like rivers than mountains, since they flow—today, with increasingly swift currents. We are beginning to be able to trace each, as a long and rich historical development over the centuries, ever accumulating, growing, changing—a dynamic reality in movement. I would return to my insistence that religious truth and falsity constitute a question pertaining to the individual men and women whose life is involved, rather than to the historical context in which they live it. The rivers and the mountains are there; some men swim in them more truly than do others, or stand more truly on some ledge. I would argue here as I have argued elsewhere, that we have to do not with religions, but with religious persons.

No person, admittedly, is religious in a vacuum. He becomes religious by participating in one or other of the historical religious traditions. Yet each man's participation is his own. And religious truth or falsity lies in that participation, rather than having been determined in advance by the institutional pattern.

Does this mean that the tradition does not matter? It would be strange indeed to argue this; when everything else matters, in impinging upon our religious living from day to day, or more accurately, on our religiously living from day to day. Religious truth is a question of persons;

yet persons are, up to a point and in part, the products of their religious system. His inherited religious structure is part of a man's environment; and is a particularly significant part, obviously, in qualifying his character and his religious life. Normally it is this that introduces him to transcendence, and serves to focus his awareness, to give shape to his intentions, to pattern his response. On a smaller scale, it would seem absurd to suggest that it does not matter religiously whether a man is a Presbyterian or a Catholic, a Mennonite farmer or a Yale Divinity School graduate student. It matters, in setting the stage on which one plays one's role; yet no man but is free to accept or to reject, to profit from or to misuse, to fall short of, to deviate from, or to transcend, the pattern of his fathers, religiously as otherwise. Life's situations and challenges are certainly significant: yet not so significant as what a man does in the face of them. To live religiously is to *live*—in a given context, yes; and the context matters, yes. Yet to *live*, at least as a human being, and especially as a religious human being *vis-à-vis* God, is to be more than simply a prisoner, a victim, an automatic reaction to, one's mundane environment.

To live a true religious life, which means to live a truly human life, which means to live a life truly responsive to God, which means to live a life truly responsive to man and to one's total situation—in short, to live truly, may be more easily done if you are brought up in one tradition than in another, just as it may be more easily done if you are poor rather than rich, or rich rather than poor, or clever rather than stupid, or humble rather than clever, or born into a godly and loving family rather than born unwanted in a broken home. No one has argued, I suppose, that all contexts are equal. All that I am arguing is that all contexts are contexts. The Hindu tradition, or that branch of it that pertains to a given village, the Buddhist tradition or some particular segment of it in the twentieth century, the Episcopalian tradition, the Shintoist—all these are various contexts in one or other of which a man is born. They are exceedingly interesting, consequential, conditioning environments. Yet religious *truth* is a function of a personal life lived in that context; not of the context itself.

This is what I mean by saying that religious traditions are simply there, like Mount Everest or the St. Lawrence River. *They* are not true, nor false; though they are certainly important.

"All right, all right," one may protest; "the religions exist, as historical facts. In their totality, maybe there is a point somewhere in what you say, that they are not simply true or false. Nonetheless some religious traditions, and conspicuously our own Christian one, in addition to providing a religious environment in which men live, also make certain statements that they claim to be true. Ours does this, and other traditions have not entirely refrained from doing the same. We believe, and want to believe, that these statements are true; or if they are not true, we want to reject or to revise them. Those claims that conflict with ours we have believed to be false. If they are not false, we want to know this; again, so that we may revise our stand. Surely you cannot deny the significance of these claims."

No, I cannot. Yet I can see complications even here. I can see persons even here. And I believe that even God sees persons primarily, even here.

Let us, then, shift gears, from the truth of religions to the truth of religious statements. This is indeed a good question; one that deserves attention, and even that deserves perhaps the new and somewhat revised attention that it is getting today. First, however, let us be clear what we are doing in making this quite serious shift.

First, as we have already remarked, not all religious traditions attempt to express themselves in verbalizations. Our Christian one does, and this is important; but let us not overestimate its centrality, even for us. William Temple has reminded us forcefully, but perhaps we must remind ourselves again and again, that the Christian revelation of God is of a person, not of propositions. Theology, he asserts, is to revelation what musical criticism is to music. Certainly it is secondary; and life certainly is sad, if one thinks to take the theoretical formulations in place of the reality. Some religious people seem to get along very well with a minimum of statement; we are too intellectualist for that, but let us not confuse the issue. Some day I should like to explore the area of faith apart from belief.

There might seem a danger here, and in all the present orientation, of anti-rationalism. This must be avoided; and can be, provided one holds fast to a firm intellectualism. For good or ill, I am a dyed-in-the-wool intellectual: a theorist by profession, by temperament, by intellectual conviction. My career is devoted to a relentless search for interpretations that will be intellectually valid; indeed, for statements that will be true, or will increasingly approximate to truth. Moreover, it is my faith (the word is deliberate) that such statements, even in the religious realm, can be found, or constructed—though not without travail. At least, I intend to go on looking, to go on trying; and I am assuming that others are equally intent. We wish to know, and we will not rest until we have hammered out theories that will fit.

However, they will still be *our* theories; in some sense, human constructs. Truth is divine; yet words are human. Even concepts are human. There is surely a limit to the capacity of words and concepts to encapsulate truth. Rather than trying to formulate that limit in words or conceptually, we may perhaps all be allowed to get by merely with the pledge that the intellectual in us will relentlessly strive for ever more adequate intellectualizations even of religious truth, without holding that the one can ever become a substitute for the other.

Returning to William Temple on theology, then, the first observation is that verbalizations are not themselves revealed, though they relate to what is (to Who is). A second perhaps follows: that their truth, too, may be related to a particular revelation, the one to which they give intellectual expression. We have said that certain religious traditions not only provide a particular religious environment in which men live; they also make certain statements, which they claim to be true. Our inquiry in the preceding chapter into the Islamic case might suggest that perhaps they are true within that environment, though not outside it. If this were so, they would serve their religious purpose. If, however, their truth were limited in this way, they would not satisfy us as intellectuals; especially if we are intellectuals outside. And if we are relentlessly intellectual, even as insiders, we are still compelled to break through limitations.

Rather than attempting any general theory, which would require at least a book, let us scrutinize one particular statement; namely, our last chapter's one: "The Qur'an is the Word of God." This has been true, perhaps, we hinted, for Muslims; false for outsiders. Can we aspire toward a statement on this topic that will hold more universally? I do so aspire. As I remarked at the time, I believe such a statement can be attained only at the end of dialogue between those who legitimately believe and those who legitimately do not. Nonetheless, let me toss in a contribution toward such a dialogue, to see what the first step from one side might be. What follows is not primarily an item for the dialogue between Christians and Muslims, but rather a preliminary step in a dialogue or colloquium first just among Christians. What is a Christian, as Christian, to do with the statement that the Qur'an is the word of God? What is he to make of it?

I see three levels at which the matter might be explored. The first is absolute and historical, the second is theological and communal, the third personalist and existential.

The first may appear at first blush altogether too naive and too simplicist. Yet I think that even this matter is really quite profound, with implications important for all of us. The point is straightforward: that any statement is the word of God insofar as it is true. One must not reject this too readily, or treat it as too insignificant, lest the

whole structure of our universe come tumbling down
about our ears. If God is not the truth, what is God, and
what is truth? But those are rhetorical questions; God *is*
truth, and one must take this intimate fact very, very
seriously. Wherever truth is found, there is God. And
wherever truth is stated, there God is speaking.

Further, some of the Qur'an is in the indicative mood,
but much of it is in the imperative: it comprises not only
statements, but especially commands. Again I would say,
wherever a right action is enjoined, there God is speaking.
Any moral injunction, insofar as it is truly moral and
correct, is the word of God.

Insofar as the Qur'an makes a statement that is true, or
a command that is just, so far it is the word of God. Have
I said anything at all here? I think so. Of course, this
definition would leave room for a difference of opinion as
to how far the statements of the Qur'an *are* true, and how
far its commands *are* just and right. On this, Muslims and,
for instance, Christians might disagree—I am not propos-
ing to abolish overnight all distinctions between the two
communities! Yet I think that I have said something quite
serious, despite appearances; something that could lead to
historical consequences far beyond any that have been
dreamed of for centuries.

Of course, there is a question of not only how true a
statement is, but also of how important; not only how
right a command, but how central. It would take us too
far afield to explore the subtle and ramifying question of
how useful or valid it may be to regard any statement,
however trivial, as the word of God insofar as it is prosaically accurate, or whether it rather can be said to become

the word of God only as it transforms personal life; let us leave that issue aside (for another time?). Yet among the Qur'an's statements, a Christian must recognize that many are very important indeed, such as that the heavens and the earth are the Lord's, that God alone is to be worshipped; and among its commands many are indeed crucial, such as "Seek justice!" I am ready to argue with all comers that the command "Seek justice!" is divine; and that any one who recognizes it as incumbent on himself, or society on itself, has taken a tremendous step, crucially important.

There are all kinds of problems here, most of which I propose to leave untouched. One, however, demands mention. Christians, affirming that the truth of God is expressed in a person, affirm concomitantly that it cannot be adequately expressed in words. I do not wish to take the edge off this point. Nonetheless, I have observed that Christians do sometimes go vastly astray with the Qur'an by not realizing that what is involved is not the words, but what the words mean. The words "Seek justice" are not dignified enough to contain divinity; but the *command* "Seek justice!" and all that that command implies, as a moral obligation impinging on man—this, in my view, is itself transcendent, infinite, and although it does not exhaust God, neither does it fail Him.

You will think of many caveats on considerations at this level; I will mention just one major limitation on it, which leads us to our second level. For omitted here is the creativity of men's response, the role of faith. Truth, both indicative and imperative, is divine; but to recognize it as divine is a further great step toward God. To be concerned with the Qur'an only insofar as it is actually true and right omits the massive religious significance of the Muslim community's regarding it as true and right—quite apart from the validity or otherwise of their judgement. Non-Muslims who do not share the verdict that this scripture is authentic, must be wary lest they miss the religious significance of such a verdict in itself.

To illustrate this important point dramatically, one might even, for the sake of argument, as the most extreme position possible, suppose that no statement in the Qur'an were true, and none of its commands right. And yet by treating it as sacrosanct, Muslims would be appropriating to themselves the foundation of all truth and all morality. Why is truth important? And why should man do his duty? Because both are from God. To recognize truth as divine, and to treat it therefore as resonantly significant, final, sacred; to recognize moral obligations as divine, and to treat them therefore as utterly inescapable, as cosmically and reverberatingly important, binding, and ultimately decisive—both these are profoundly correct apprehensions. God is indeed saying this to man, so that even if the book in which He were recognized as saying it contained no actual truth, no right imperative, even so it would at this level be the word of God.

The Muslim community has held that the Qur'an, the word of God, is uncreated, eternal; that that word is an attribute of God Himself, not something different from Him. A Christian, while he may differ as to the Qur'an's filling this role, must not fail to recognize that the Muslim community, in positing that such a role is there to be filled, is making a valid and important point. To say that the Qur'an is the word of God in this sense, is to say, among other things, that God is not quiet, passive, inscrutable, but that He speaks: He is a God who from all eternity and by His very nature has something to say to man, that He is the kind of God who takes the initiative to say it—that religious history is not, therefore, man's seeking after God but is rather God's seeking after man, and that what is required is man's response to God's initiative.

If you as a Christian meet two members of the Muslim community, one of whom is a sceptic, saying that all this is nonsense, that the Qur'an is a purely mundane book written in the seventh century by a chap called Muhammad, and that if there be a God, which he doubts, certainly there is no communication between that God and mankind; while the other member of the community says no, that God is speaking here, meaning by that *inter alia* what we have just said about God's initiative and communication and human response and responsibility and the like—then you as a Christian must recognize that the second man is closer to the truth than is the first. Of the two religious positions, the one that holds the Qur'an to be the word of God is more true than the one that holds it not to be, you as a Christian must affirm. The validity of part of your Christian faith is at stake here: not *against* but *for* the Muslim answer to our question.

This level, too, of consideration is seriously limited, however. For like the first, though less so, it suffers from what seems a fundamental fallacy in all this realm; namely, that of treating these questions in abstract or generalized terms, rather than in the only terms that count or that are relevant, which are personal ones. This is the third level at which we should consider our proposition. Let me illustrate it with a story.

Once I was climbing in the Himalayas, not far from a settlement but along a track somewhat remote, and came across a fruit seller, a humble and poor and loveable old man with a stack of oranges that he was selling by weight, at so many *annās* per *sīr,* or we might say at so many cents per pound. For scales he had a rough and ready balance, consisting of two pans suspended by strings attached at each end of a rough crossbar. The bar he held in his hand suspended by a string from its mid-point. He put oranges in one pan and weighed them against some rocks that he had there, a middle-sized one and two smallish ones the three of which together made up one *sīr* (two pounds). He was too poor to own metal weights, stamped and standard. That the three stones actually weighed a *sīr* was an unverified presumption; though I personally believe that they did. I watched him for a while, as he made occasional sales to passers-by; and afterwards fell into conversation with him. He was far from any possibility of having his dealings checked; and there was no external measure of his honesty, which I found was sustained rather by a verse from the Qur'an which runs "Lo! He over all things is watching."

Now because he believed the Qur'an to be the word of God, that verse ringing in his ears from memory signified to him that God Himself was watching him and was telling him to be honest. Now I submit that in that situation, God *was* in fact that particular afternoon speaking to that particular shriveled old man in the words of the Qur'an—

or through the words of the Qur'an, if you prefer. His faith made it come alive to him; and his faith, I submit, did not deceive him. You and I need not be Muslim to recognize that in such a situation God can indeed speak to man. This incident happened in July, 1943. It happened at a particular moment, at a particular place, in the life of a particular person. This is what is meant by saying that God speaks to man, if it means anything at all: that He speaks to real men, in real situations, in actual living encounter.

To say that the Qur'an is the word of God is to say something about 1943, or 1967, and not primarily about the seventh century in Arabia when Muhammad was alive. I therefore feel that it is misleading and false to ask whether the Qur'an is the word of God in general, absolutely and impersonally; and to look back into the remote past for an answer. I have known situations where it was not the word of God, and I have known other situations where it was. An example of the former is an undergraduate last term who found it tedious and uncouth: God did not speak through the Qur'an to her, though He does speak through it to other persons—chiefly Muslims, of course: it is evident enough that here as elsewhere faith, if not a prerequisite, is at any rate virtually a condition of God's acting. To those that believe that He will speak or is speaking, apparently He can speak. I should not like to say that He cannot to others, but it would seem that normally He does not. This is empirical observation, not theological speculation.

Therefore, instead of saying that the Qur'an is (or, again, is not) the word of God, we should rather, so far as

I can discern, say that the Qur'an was the word of God to al-Ghazzali, it was the word of God yesterday morning to Muslim Q who was at that point warned or inspired or challenged by it; it was *not* that word yesterday afternoon to that same Muslim Q because by then he had forgotten it, and it was not the word of God to Carlyle or Tillich and is not to de Gaulle. I personally can go further and say that it was not the word of God to Muslim Y on a certain day in such-and-such a year when he understood (misunderstood?) it to be saying to him that he should go and chop off the heads of certain Hindus. So far, these are all historical statements. For a Muslim they can become existential ones. He may, for instance, believe that the Qur'an is the word of God abstractly, but pray that it may become so concretely and personally now as he is about to read it. And if he were sufficiently sophisticated and modern and informed and critical, he could even omit the abstraction and deal only in terms of the immediate and personal situation. He need not say or believe that the Qur'an is the word of God, provided he can say, and believe, and pray that it may become so, for him, today.

I do not know how shocked some may be if I apply this same sort of reasoning to our Christian case. Rather than saying that Jesus Christ is the full revelation of God, I would say rather that He is a revelation of God to me, and has been to many other people, though I know others to whom He has not been. I can quite truthfully say that Christ reveals God to me more fully today than He did twenty years ago, and can sincerely pray that this will become more true. It is an empirical observation, whether the facts ought to have been so or not, that thirty years ago, when I was a questioning undergraduate in the Depression, God spoke to me more effectively through the words of Amos than He did through Christ. This was not so ten years earlier, nor fifteen years later; but it was so then.

When I say that Christ reveals God to me more fully today than He did twenty years ago, and when I pray that it may become more true tomorrow, of these statements I know both the meaning and the truth. I do not know quite what it might mean to speak of a revelation of God in general without some person to whom He is revealed. I rather wonder whether we have not got ourselves into considerable difficulty by thinking in those de-personalized terms. We have allowed ourselves to speak of revelation as if the term had meaning when it has a subject, rather than recognizing that meaning for it requires both a subject and an object. Just as there can be no revelation that is not a revelation of something (or someone), so there can be none that is not a revelation *to* someone. There is no revelation of God except to particular persons.

To come back to our word-of-God concept, let us shift from the empirical historical approach that I have been using to a more theological one. I may speak as a Christian minister, to Christian ministers; and may relate my empirical observations to Christian theology. It is a matter of historical observation when I say that, so far as I can see, God spoke to al-Ghazzali in the words of the Qur'an. I come to this conclusion by reading al-Ghazzali's books, and studying his life. Yet I come to it also by being Christian. It coheres more closely with what I know of

God as revealed to me in Christ, and as instructed to me in Christian theology, to say that presumably God is, as it were, trying to speak to men in love and justice and mercy wherever they may be, in and through whatever context in which they may find themselves; and that in the case of Muslims he reaches out to them through the Islamic religious tradition and particularly the words of the Qur'an. That He makes use of man's religious symbols in His initiative in coming to them, not exclusively but largely, would seem evident and understandable. Apart from some doctrine of predestination (I was brought up a Calvinist), a Christian cannot but believe, surely, that God's speaking to Muslims through the Qur'an is limited perhaps partly by the form of the Qur'an and partly by the capacity of the individual Muslim to respond; but is not limited on God's side.

So far as the Qur'an in seventh-century Arabia is concerned, then, I would supersede the two traditional answers that we discussed in our last chapter (that it is, and that it is not, the word of God) by saying that the Qur'an was the word of Muhammad, historically conditioned, and that it was at the same time—being in some measure transcendently true—the closest approximation to the eternal word of God to which Muhammad was capable of rising; and that since that time, thanks to the place that it has been given in the Islamic religious tradition, it has become and continues to be the word of God to many Muslims, varying in authenticity and largeness and intimacy from person to person and from hour to hour: that sometimes it is more, sometimes less, sometimes not at all, but that the history of the Muslim community cannot be understood without a recognition that it has so served—and that indeed without that recognition neither can one understand the dealings of God with the sons of men outside the visible Church.

Another way of phrasing this same point is perhaps simpler, though its implications reach just as far, in all directions. Might we say that the statement "the Qur'an is the word of God," rather than being in itself true or false, at a generic or abstract level, impersonally, can become true—in the life of a particular person; and further, that it has become true in the lives of many persons; and further, that it has become more true in the lives of certain persons, at certain times, than others. It becomes true through faith. (It can also become false.)

I leave with you the question as to whether this applies to all religious statements, including our Christian ones: that they have become true for some men, and that they may become true for me, that they may become more true for me than they yet have.

If this were so, another question would perhaps follow; namely, can some religious statements become more true than others? To discuss this collaboratively would open up the possibility of a new era, perhaps, in inter-community discourse and inter-community understanding. I would still insist that we relate it to the lives and the faith of persons.

We may answer our last chapter's question, then, by saying that the Qur'an has become the word of God to some men, not to others—and of the former, those to whom it has become so, it has become so more truly to some than to others.

Now the interesting things about this type of answer are two. The first is that this way of looking at the matter appears, to me at last, as observer and theorist, to be nearer the truth; and my argument has endeavored to make this persuasive. True statements, in the religious realm, are significant and are worth striving after—even if they are not as important as, or anyway are not a substitute for, true lives.

The second point is that this type of statement would seem potentially capable of being accepted eventually by both Muslims and Christians.

The two points are, of course, related. So long as we disagree, one at least of us is wrong; or, both are inadequate. And there is perhaps some reason to imagine that the latter is the case. Contrariwise, if anyone can really arrive at a statement that approximates the truth, then both groups of us, both desiring the truth, should be able and happy to adopt it.

Probably I have failed. Yet even if, in the process, I have illustrated what is required, that in itself may be an advance.

IV CHRISTIAN—
NOUN,
OR
ADJECTIVE?

Christian—Noun, or Adjective?

If someone comes up to me and asks if I am a Christian (as, for instance, in India the Census agents used to do), I find it easy to answer "yes," in a glib sort of way, and then turn back to getting on with my job. The question is easy, the answer is straightforward, and the matter is quickly settled.

If, on the other hand, someone asks me if I am Christian, the situation changes radically. This I find a searching question, and disquieting; one that undermines my complacency. Indeed, to ponder it is to be set all a-tremble. The question is not easy; nor is the answer straightforward. Obviously it is not a yes-or-no matter; the question ought rather to be, "How Christian are you?" I cannot answer by confidently laying claim to any large share of Christian-ness ("Oh, I am very Christian indeed, thank you very much") for that would be both arrogant, and false. Yet neither can I absolve myself by confessing that, alas, I am hardly Christian at all; for I may recognize how little Christian I really am and yet I am haunted by a powerful sense that I ought to be more Christian than that. A high answer is pretentious; a low answer is just not good enough. Something in between has the faults of both these. In fact, I just cannot answer the question at all.

Yet, neither can I dismiss it. Once it is put to me, it goes on probing my conscience, in dynamic restlessness—spurring me, let us hope, to a life not of much or of little but of the pilgrimage of always *more*.

This dynamic quality is significant: the matter varies, from day to day. The first of our two questions need be asked, normally, only once: short of an unlikely upheaval, a tick in the appropriate column of the Census report will carry over from one survey to another. Some of my friends have not changed their street address in the past ten years; it so happens that I have; but almost none of us has changed his formal "religion." If a man asked me "Are you a Christian?" last autumn, I should not expect him to repeat the question this spring, unless he had forgotten. "Am I Christian?" however, is far from being so settled an issue. Perhaps yesterday morning for a brief spell I was indeed fairly Christian in my treatment of my fellow passengers as I got into a train; but I was perhaps not Christian in the evening at rush hour. How Christian was I last spring when I voted in the Canadian elections, on the issue, among others, of nuclear weapons? Do you find, perhaps, that there are certain persons with whom you are usually less Christian in your dealings than with others? Nor are the issues only moral: it is a deep, persistent question how Christian am I as I excogitate a doctrinal interpretation. Was I truly Christian as I wrote the last chapter? Was the Church truly Christian when it formulated the Westminster Confession? How Christian are we as we hammer out a new theology of comparative religion?

Let me illustrate the matter in another way. A few

years ago I was walking with friends in the Laurentian hills north of Montreal, soon after I came to those parts; and we came across a resort lodge which bore to my surprise a placard declaring: "For Christians Only." I remarked on this, curious at what I took to be an evangelical or fundamentalist commericalism; my naïvité was rebuked by my being informed by my laughing friends that this simply indicated that Jews were not admitted.

I was shocked, first at the discrimination, but perhaps more profoundly at the self-righteousness of its excuse. That wickedness can be labeled "Christian" is educative. Although I did not think of it at the time, my present point is nicely set forth here. For clearly no sensitive or decent Christian could patronize that hotel. That particular day our party had been hiking for a few pleasant hours through the woods, and it had vaguely crossed my mind when we saw this establishment a piece off that we might stop in for afternoon tea. When we saw the sign, however, it was clear that we could not enter. An hotel that excludes those that are not Christians, by the same act excludes those that are Christian. Noun and adjective are here torn laceratingly apart.

The noun is comforting, the adjective demanding. The noun is static, the adjective dynamic. The noun asserts, the adjective pleads. The noun is human, the adjective divine.

At the beginning, there was sensitivity in this matter: when the affair first arose, in Antioch. Our term, one recalls, from the Bible, developed there. As with other names designating members of a new or newly encountered religious community—"Quaker," "Pietist," "Metho-

dist," "Muhammadan," "Hindu," "Buddhist," "Confucian,"
"Shintoist"—so this term, too, was introduced by outsiders; not without a touch of the outsider's disdain. The
Roman Empire called the disciples *Christianoi,* at Antioch. Members of the Church itself, we are told, at first resisted the appelation. The reason for this was manifestly
their sensitive embarrassment. We do not deserve, they
were saying in effect, to be called Christ-like, Christ-ish,
Messianic.

Today we have got so used to the term over the inter-
vening centuries, have become so accustomed to bandying
it about carelessly, irreverently, that we have lost not only
their hesitation, but even any clear grasp of why they
should be hesitant. St. Ignatius, however, makes it clear.
He was Bishop of that same Antioch toward the end of
the first century; and early in the second was martyred,
under the persecution of Trajan. His extant letters were
written while he was on his way to Rome to be put to
death. In those days, one must remember, the term designated not those who have privileged entry to exclusive
country clubs, but those whom the Empire marked out for
throwing to the lions. Yet we are not worthy of it, said
those to whom the word applied. Ignatius, however,
replies in effect: All right, let us accept the name; not as
something of which we are worthy, but as something to
which we may aspire. They will put me to death because
they say I am *Christianos.* I hope that I may be found
so—not only in name, but in fact.[1] It would add quite a
new quality to our thinking, and perhaps to our living, if
we today recaptured his notion that being martyred may

[1] His *Letter to the Romans,* Chap. 3, verse 3.

perhaps justify a little more the otherwise undeserved application to us of the term "Christian," which to him evidently meant "Christ-like." If you will die for your faith, perhaps you will deserve the name; but hardly otherwise!

One of the leading motifs of his thought is his concept of *mathēsis*, also *mimēsis*, of Christ: the *imitatio Christi*. In *Philadelphians* 7:2, for example, he writes: "Become imitators of Jesus Christ, just as He is of His Father." By this standard, how many of us are Christian?

And yet dare we reject this standard?

In passing, one may perhaps note that in Greek and Latin, adjectives as well as nouns are declined for the plural, unlike English; so that the distinction that I am making here is left to the subtlety and appreciation of the reader, rather than being externalized in the phrasing. This means that translators are free to choose, after exercising their imagination—or even, perhaps, before or without exercising it. The text in Acts 11:26 says in Greek that the disciples were called first in Antioch *Christianoi*. This could be rendered into English "were called Christian," though the King James' version translates ". . . were called Christians . . ."; and subsequent versions have followed this in the cases that I have looked up, including the New English Bible. It would make a nice little exercise to investigate this particular point more thoroughly than I have done.

I have investigated with some care certain facets of the evolving history of the use of the adjective; and have discovered some quite startling matters. It is a highly rewarding exercise to inquire a little discerningly what vari-

ous writers have meant when they said "Christian"; just as
it can prove a highly rewarding, perhaps purifying, disci-
pline, to ask *oneself* what one means, or proposes to mean,
by it—not merely when one is about to use it in speech or
in writing, although that could be richly worthwhile; but
also when one is not. In the silence of one's room, in the
hub-bub of the melée, in the busy current of one's routine
or in one's crises, there would surely be value in reflecting
on what "Christian" might mean right then and there.
Each morning as one arises, one might well ask oneself
what one intends to make this word mean for oneself that
day.

I should like next to divert attention to certain parallels
to this situation in the case of other communities; and to
certain complications that then arise cross-culturally, to
elaborate and enrich our understanding.

First, a similar ambiguity can be detected in, for instance, the Islamic case. There, as with us in the Church,
the word "Muslim" is used both as noun and as adjective:
the noun formal, mundane, designating membership in an
historical community as an external fact, while the adjective refers to content, to a relationship of man to heaven,
designating an internal attitude and orientation. Ask a
member of the Islamic community if he is "a Muslim,"
and he can answer "yes" in a forthright manner, losing no
sleep over the problem and giving it no prior and no subsequent thought. He tosses out the answer, proudly, no
doubt, but then goes on with his work. Ask him, however,
if he is *muslim*, and he must be quite insensitive to words
or else to responsibilities if he can answer glibly and with-

out a reverent trepidation. "Muslim" is Arabic for "sub-mitter" or "self-committing," so that to affirm that a person is *muslim* is to speak of his quality of heart, his commitment to God, his readiness to obey whatever injunctions the moral law may make incumbent on him. Two men may both be Muslims, but one of them may be more *muslim* than the other, may be more *muslim* in one situation than in another, more *muslim* one afternoon than the next morning.

In classical Islamic theology, one of the points on which two schools divided was the question of whether it is legitimate for a man to say "I am one who has faith, in very truth," or whether he must rather say "I am one who has faith, if God will." The term here was not *muslim*, which on the whole seems a relatively modern usage in its widespread form, but the earlier counterpart *mu'min;* but the point at issue was virtually the same. I have not actually read in Islamic literature any discussion exactly along the lines that I am suggesting here (I have not read a counterpart exactly in Christian literature either, for that matter); but those Muslims who hesitated to lay unconditional claim to the characterization *mu'min,* sensing the pretension, and also those who even appreciated the discussion, I should expect to understand my argument, just as I expect sensitive Christians to understand it. *Islam,* the verbal noun of which *muslim* is the participle, means pristinely "surrender," "commitment," the active giving of oneself to obedience to God's claims, the positive response to God's initiative. The theologians also discussed whether it was the same thing as *faith* (most said that it was, though their argument never fully satisfied, so that the issue continued to be canvassed), and whether faith is an *either/or* matter, or can be more or less. These became technical and elaborate discussions, and I do not wish to go into them here; but I think that I am not being extravagant in making the point that Muslims know very well what it is to be more or to be less devout. (The words "devout" and "Muslim"—that is, the English word "devout" and the Arabic word "Muslim"—are etymologically closely parallel.) And the Sufis among them, at least, have felt that the significant and searching question is not "Are you a Muslim?" but "How *muslim* are you?"—or, more ultimately and tremulously, "How Muslim am I?"

When Abraham is commanded by God, in order to test his faith, to sacrifice his son, he hesitates for a brief moment of alarm in the vivid Qur'anic story but quickly acquiesces, so that at that moment he once again becomes *muslim* adjectivally, as does his son who also "submits" ("devoutly") to the injunction.[2] This Arabic word is used. Abraham and his son (Ishmael, in the later Islamic version) were not nominal MUSLIMS at all, were not Musalmans, were certainly not Muhammadans. They were *muslim* in the Arabic sense of the word; were characterized, or rather characterized themselves, or rather were granted by God the grace of becoming characterized, by this participle or verbal adjective.

To take another scriptural figure, might one say that the Good Samaritan was not a Christian, but was Christian?

However that may be, or the case of Abraham as a non-Muslim *muslim*, let us consider a modern involvement. I

[2] Qur'an 37:102 ff.

said that there were cross-cultural implications that complicate and enrich this whole matter.

I personally am not a Muslim. Perhaps relatively few of my readers will be. Again, my answer to a question on this point can be quick, clear, and definite. Yet if the question is raised, am I Muslim, the answer is not quick nor clear nor definite. Normally I do not talk Arabic nor do my hearers listen to that language; but here is an adjective from it, and the question is, does it apply to me, or can I apply it to myself. The only possible answer that I can give to this question is that I hope so. Any other would be blasphemous and arrogant. I try to be as muslim as I can; as obedient to God's demands; as ready as He gives me the grace to be, to submit to His direction. I am not, alas, in the practice of my life, as *muslim* as a good Christian should be. But certainly I aspire to be. Those of you whose hearts God has opened to surrender [3] normally do not think in terms of this particular adjective to characterize the quality of your orientation; but whether you know it or not, this adjective describes the attitude to which in your best moments you hope to rise.

A man cannot be both a Christian and a Muslim at the same time. The nouns keep us apart. On the other hand, it is not, I suggest, as ridiculous or fanciful as might be supposed, to ask whether in the realm of adjectives it may not be possible for a man to be both Christian and Muslim at the same time. I for one can understand and countenance meanings for the terms in which not only is this possible, but even in which one could say that to be truly Christian is *ipso facto* to be truly *muslim*.

[3] This wording is from the Qur'an (39:22).

I can also understand and even sympathize with, even if finally I cannot countenance, other meanings for these terms in accord with which this statement would not be valid; and others in accord with which it would not even be understood. Maybe you misunderstand it—certainly you do if you feel that it is saying anything with which St. Ignatius would not agree. My concept is quite orthodox; it is only the terminology that is brash. Lest one think all this but a clever *tour de force,* however, let me give another quite unrelated example.

One of the things that has burned itself most deeply into my consciousness is the Hindu-Muslim cataclysm of 1947, the time of the partition of India: the terrifying upheaval of hatred and violence, when ten million persons were uprooted and perhaps one million were massacred, many brutally. I neither underestimate nor forget, then, that Muslims are not Hindus. Between these two groups the difference is stark, the gulf deep, the hostility explosive. You may note that the groups are designated by the noun: Muslims, and Hindus. As I have said, Muslims are not Hindus—emphatically not, drastically not, searingly not.

If we shift to adjectives, however, the dichotomy begins to dissolve. The word "Hindu" is, originally, an adjective; and means, originally, "Indian." It is used as an adjective in this geographical and comprehensive sense as recently as the nineteenth century, and even into the twentieth. One finds this usage in Persian poetry, for instance; and also in Urdu poetry, including that written by Muslims. Nor is it unknown in Western languages, into quite recent times. The only meaning given for *Hindou,* in my French dictionary, the 1932 edition of *Nouveau Petit Larousse,* is "of Hindustan" ("de l'Hindoustan"); and its article *Art Hindou* embraces the whole of Indian art, and includes something on the special Islamic forms, including mosques. I can remember as a boy in Canada we used to distinguish between Red Indians and Hindu Indians, meaning by the latter simply "Indians from India." More recently I have heard the phrase *Hindu* Muslims as distinct from *Arab* Muslims and *Turkish* Muslims; I have even met this usage, in English, on the lips of Near Eastern Muslims. And indeed not too long ago this was current, I have found, among Muslims of India themselves, strange though it seem today. It is not impossible to find a nineteenth-century Urdu verse in which the Muslim poet writes "We Hindu Musulmans," meaning "We Muslims of India." Sir Sayyid Ahmad Khan, founder of the present Muslim University at Aligarh, and the Indo-Muslim community's outstanding leader and chief spokesman in the last quarter of last century, said in a speech in Allahabad: "We Muslims of this country, we too are Hindu." I do not think that it would be possible to say this today, after all the turmoil and bitterness, after the definition of the nouns in bloodshed; is it conceivable, perhaps, that it may at some time in the future again become possible? The twentieth-century poet Iqbal, the ideological founder of Pakistan, wrote in his youth, "We are Hindī," using an adjective only slightly divergent.

It would seem, then, that there are many and diverse instances where adjectives are less exclusivist, less divisive, less arrayed for battle, than are nouns. Nouns are black and white; adjectives are a rainbow spectrum of color.

In the Indian/Hindu case I have touched on the matter of historical evolution; and this, of course, is not chance. The principle applies also in the other cases; one can trace for each a gradual externalization, institutionalization, secularization, over the centuries. Let us return to the Christian instance. We saw that with St. Ignatius, and the same is true for all the early writers that I have consulted, the term "Christian" signifies "pertaining to Christ." Gradually, however, one can discern the rise of a new meaning, where "Christian" signifies "pertaining to Christians." The transition is subtle, and often passes unnoticed; but no Christian can be so arrogant as not to recognize that the difference is radical. The "Christian quarter" of a town may indicate nothing more than that it is inhabited by a number of persons who are nominally Christians, people like me and my fellows who may be Christians only in the sense that we are not Jews, nor Buddhists. Our section of town might become Christian in certainly a deeper, certainly a different, sense, if we persons who inhabited it could rise to being Christian, and not merely Christians. One may remember the Fellowship for a Christian Social Order. Some of us tried once to do our little bit to make life Christian in that significant sense; and in this realm of meaning, it is possible to think of a section of a town becoming *Christian*. However, it would require a good deal of effort, and not a little grace, to make a quarter Christian in that sense; whereas with no effort at all, and perhaps even no grace at all, it can be labeled Christian in the other.

Similarly there is a Christian arrogance, of which Jews, and South African negroes, and Asians are conscious: the arrogance of Christians. And there is Christian humility: the humility of Christ. Not to sense the difference between these is gross. In this radical see-saw back-and-forth of adjectival reference, one can speak of Christian insensitivity, and of Christian sensitivity: the one mundane, the other transcendent; the one what is, the other what ought to be; the one to bewail, the other to pray for. Thus, too: Christian injustice to minorities, and Christian justice to minorities. Along this line, it is possible and meaningful to ask, how Christian is Christian practice, how Christian are Christian theories, even how Christian is the Christian Church.

In this connection, one must note that outsiders, failing to catch the transcendent reference of the ideal use, are usually limited to the mundane antecedents; so that Europe normally uses the adjective "Muslim" to signify what pertains to the noun "Muslim," to the Muslims, rather than what pertains to God—just as Jews tend to hear the adjective "Christian" as referring to us, rather than to Christ.

I dream that this need not be so. A great step forward would be taken in inter-community understanding and awareness, if we could learn to recognize the transcendence of each other's aspiration. It will help our own religious life, I am contending, if we rise to a true apprehension of the dynamic and divine quality of our own adjectives. Concomitantly, it will help to make possible broth-

erhood and concord, if, for every community's religiousness, we can come to recognize that adjectives come before nouns. I said that it is not meaningless to ask, how
Christian is the Christian Church. It requires a person
imaginative and sensitive to ask, how Buddhist are the
Buddhists—but asking it will be an act of true insight and
of creative sympathy. As St. Ignatius recognized that we
would, we Christians have failed to live up to the name by
which we live. So, too, have Muslims: like the rest of us
they have fallen short of the principle that informs them,
so that it becomes significant and even helpful to ask, how
Muslim is the Muslim community. We shall appreciate
them more truly if we ask this. The religious life of all
mankind is to be rightly understood only in terms of adjectives, not nouns.

In our preceding chapter, we wrestled for a time with
certain questions of truth and falsehood in religion.
Clearly there are many problems unresolved in that
realm, and there will still be many tomorrow. However,
perhaps I may for a moment touch on a certain relationship between the concept of truth and the conception of
religious life as adjectival. I argued there that religions
are not propositions and therefore cannot be true and
false in that particular sense of those terms. However, this
is not the only sense in which truth is to be conceived.
The propositional notion of truth and falsehood, as attrib-
utes of statements, has tended to dominate Western
thought since the Enlightenment. The re-awakening, however, of our awareness that faith is not a belief in theories,
that God has given to us for our salvation not a doctrinal

system, should have alerted us more effectively than has sometimes been the case, to a deeper understanding also of truth itself. Perhaps science has dazzled us a little too much here, since scientists are good at theories and statements, which they themselves do not rush to call "true" but which philosophers find easy to handle and very well behaved, a model perhaps for man's other children. Impersonal truth perhaps lends itself to statement form, but personal truth appears of another quality. At least, there would seem occasion to consider for a moment the relation of truth to adjectives.

Let us reflect on such an assertion as "Christian marriage is true marriage." The matter is complicated because I believe this assertion itself to be true, as well as the marriage that it is talking about; but I will deliberately evade such complications. It is perhaps useful to note certain negative points: things that this dictum does not tell us. For example, if Christian marriage is true marriage, it does not follow that all Christians are truly married. In this last, note the noun: all *Christians*. From the truth of an adjective, nothing follows about nouns. The actual behavior of two real live Christians in historical situations cannot sully or infringe the purity and truth of the affirmation, of which their behavior may be independent. One could infer, on the other hand, from this equation, and one would be surely right, that how Christian a man adjectivally is, has something to say about the quality of his marriage. The proposition here is general and abstract, as heavenly as one could well wish: "Christian marriage is true marriage." Yet with this generic and timeless ideal is related directly an immediate, concrete, historical actuality, the quality of your marriage or mine last Saturday, or in relation to particular children, in terms of our Christianness. The truth of an adjective is more important, it would seem, and more meaningful, than is the play of nouns.

Again, the asseveration "Christian marriage is true marriage" can be put with whatever vigor and reiteration one may choose; but it tells us nothing about Buddhist marriage. If it does not follow at once that all Christians are truly married, neither does it follow that all Buddhists are falsely so. One may hold the conviction with full heart, and yet not be at all uncomfortable at the thought that some Buddhists may be, and no doubt are, truly married. The pronouncement may first have been formulated, as is actually the case with all these formulations, with Buddhists not at all in mind; in fact, before those concerned knew anything at all about Buddhists. When one does hear about that community, however, and perhaps has Buddhist friends whose marriage is a delight, one welcomes this, with a warm and genuine welcome. Again, the adjective is more friendly: productive not of frontiers but of universal human qualities. There is no earthly reason, and certainly no heavenly reason, why one should not hold that "Christian marriage is true marriage" and "Buddhist marriage is true marriage" at the same time.

Similarly, you may believe that Christian courage is true courage, without holding that every Christian is of course truly courageous, and without holding that every Buddhist is *a priori* frightened. You cannot believe it, however, and hold yourself to be very Christian if in fact you are desolately scared. The proposition becomes a guide to your living, in terms of day-to-day quality; but not a guide to your sitting in judgement on men, in terms of a chess-board of wooden figures marshalled in rows for conflict.

And so it goes. I am seriously suggesting that our religious life would be deepened and made more true, and our relations with our fellows would be sweetened and made more human, if we could learn always to think of "Christian" and the rest as primarily adjectives.

Rather than continuing to explore this matter with further examples and in further ramification, can we summarize the thesis in an intelligible overall position? For the matter is not a linguistic trick; nor am I one of those who hold that philosophy is but glorified grammar. The point is a truly religious one; and as I say, a serious one. Yet also it is relatively simple. It rests, in fact, on the quiet, but firm, basis that true religion is a quality of personal living; that whatever else it be, religious life is a kind of life. It is a relation—a living relation—between man and God; an actual relation, new every morning, between particular, real men, in concrete, changing situations, and God. Not a relation between man and ideas; nor between man and institutions; not between man and types, nor between types and God. It is a relation of knowing and loving, mutually, personally.

This knowing of God, and loving Him, however, involve also knowing and loving our neighbor—who also can be known and loved only as a person, not as a type. We might equally have said, true religion is a relation between man and man: a living relation; an actual relation, new every morning, among particular, real men in concrete, changing situations. We *believe*, as Christians, that

our neighbor is a person, a child of God, and that we
ought to love him; but our *knowing* that he is (as distinct
from believing it) and our loving him (as distinct from
feeling that we ought to love him), are questions of how
Christian (adjectively) we really are, so as to see him as a
person rather than being distracted into thinking of him
as a Muslim or a Buddhist or a Jew—and thus seeing, not
him as he personally is, but an image of him that has been
abstractly constructed. He is a person qualified, as are all
persons, by character, and context; so that an endless
series of adjectives applies, some of them exceedingly
significant—yet none of them superhuman so as to usurp
his personality, and become a noun. To know men in love,
is a quality of our life as persons, as of theirs, and therefore adjectival to us both. It is a manner of our living together; it is a way, the true way, of being human.

If any entities (nouns) stand, then, between us and our
neighbor, we are not yet fully Christian. If any entities are
conceptualized between us and our neighbor, our thinking is not adequately Christian.

Moreover God Himself, we know, is a person. I say "we
know," but that too needs bringing alive: we may *believe*
it, by being Christians, but *knowing* it is a question of our
being Christian; and the more Christian we are, the more
we genuinely know it, not as a belief in theory but as a
living awareness in practice of encounter. Knowing God is
an adjectival quality of our life as persons. It is a manner
of living. It is a way, the true way, of being human.

If any entities stand between us and God, then we are
not yet fully Christian. If any entities are conceptualized
between us and God, then our thinking is not adequately

Christian. Nouns describe things in this world. Man, however, alone among the things in this world, is so constructed that he is not limited to this world, though he lives and acts within it. God has made us for Himself; so that we are open, without ceasing to be human, to be transformed back into His image. This is true of man as such, not a particular type of man. The only nouns are "God" and "person"; all else is adjective.

This is a principle not of grammar but of metaphysics. It is a truth not of language but of Christian life.

This is all very well, some may say; but what about the saving act of Christ? Is my exposition not at heart Pelagian? To be a Christian in this adjectival sense is doubtless good—as the Muslim mystic has put it: become qualified with the qualities of God. Yet the central experience of the Christian Church has cautioned that to aim at righteousness is self-defeating, and it has proclaimed that sinners are saved in a once-for-all and simple act of faith. Does my analysis neglect this Crux?

Behind my being Christian, stands the fact of my having undertaken to be Christian. Is my commitment to follow Christ not prior to my following of him? And though my following wavers from day to day, and limps, and even fails, yet my decision, taken once, and God's acceptance of it, stand firm. Are we not judged by our faith, not our works?

Now it is true that no Buddhist succeeds, I suppose, in really being Buddhist, in being Buddha-like. Indeed, one might perhaps define a Buddhist not by what he is, but by what he aims at being. Those are Buddhist whose intention is to become Buddhist; Muslim is he that commits himself to being Muslim. Muslims differ among themselves in the sincerity, perseverance, and effectiveness with which they actually live the Muslim life. What they have in common is the engagement to take it on, the acceptance of God's offer of salvation through living this way, within the community of others who have accepted. Salvation comes not, the theologians argue, from living Muslimly, but from recognizing the authenticity, the divine provenance, the incumbency, of this way of living, and saying "yes" to it. Salvation in the Islamic case, the community avers, is by faith, not by works. The crucial point in the Christians' life, the evangelists remind us, is our decision to live it: a Christian is one who accepts. The question of how one responds, is subordinate to the ultimate question of whether.

This problem is serious; but I think not so clear-cut as has sometimes been argued. If I wished just to score a debating point, I might urge that yes, my intention to be Christian takes precedence over my success in acting upon it, and yet that even that intention is really adjectival. Not only the Christian quality of my life varies from day to day, but even the force and significance, and even the fact, of my intention to maintain it. To accept Christ I do not find quite so neat a yes-or-no matter as some seem to, nor so tidy a once-for-all matter. My acceptance varies in quality and depth, in awareness and sincerity, even perhaps in fact. I do not wish to revive old controversies about the perseverance of the saints, and backsliding. Yet surely one will understand what is meant if I contend that the degree to which I accept Christ is itself a significant question.

My intention precedes my execution. Yet, how serious is my intention, how profound, how all-embracing? And how sustained is it?

The point is too serious, however, to be argued; it needs rather, I feel, to be discussed. To such a discussion I would wish to contribute my sense that even our response is a continuing matter, and that the quality of it is a personal characteristic.

There is, too, the quite massive consideration here that ultimately the response is to God: for us Christians, *through* Christ, yet not simply *to* Christ but to God. Sometimes this has been under-emphasized or forgotten —but with disastrous consequences. For we must remember that for many men and women on earth the response to God has been through other channels. (And I say "We must" here, with all the force of Christian involvement.) If anyone hold that there is no response to God outside the Christian tradition, I would urge that he is, simply, wrong. If anyone holds that the only response to God that matters, or that saves, is to God in Jesus Christ, then I would answer that even this (though I disagree with it) is to affirm that the ultimate, cosmic question is how men respond to God, not whether.

It may even be—and I should like to see this pondered and discussed—that there is indeed a final dichotomy among men on this "whether": that preceding all adjectives characterizing the quality and the manner of one's responding, there are the *either/or* nouns, two cosmic types: those who respond, and those who spurn. Zarathustra tended to think of two such types, and this dualism has had no doubt a mighty history. I personally

matizing of a point, rather than a cold scien-
nt describing our human situation: poetry
than prose, provocative rather than conclusive. In
any case, this much is surely clear: that those among us,
and those among the Muslims and others, who wish to
maintain this metaphysics of dichotomy must certainly
now revise it so as to draw the frontier of the saved and
the damned in some other way than to coincide with the
boundary of one's own historico-religious community. If
there are two categories of men on earth, ultimate and
cosmic—two categories, that is, in the eyes of God—even
so the nouns to describe them we have not yet discovered.
I do not feel confident that "Christians and non-Chris-
tians," or "Muslims and non-Muslims," will do. (Neither,
surely, will "religious" and "irreligious"; though these are
adjectives.) If God sees us all as basically in one or other
of two types, there is scriptural ground (in both Qur'an
and Bible) for imagining that even He is waiting until the
Day of Judgement to make up His mind.

Over against this I myself tend to feel, both from my
observation of the religious history of mankind throughout the world, and from my contemplation of God in the
face of Jesus on the Cross, that the human response to
God is not *either/or* so much as qualitative. I wonder
whether there is any human being on earth who does not
respond to God at all, at all. It has been said that the only
true atheist is he who loves no one and whom no one
loves; who sees no beauty, feels no justice, seeks no truth,
knows no joy, has no hope. God finds some of us pretty
tough to reach, I guess; but He leaves perhaps none of us
totally untouched by His grace and splendor.

For the Christian, the dilemma might be pointed in this way. I said at the beginning of this chapter that basically one cannot oneself give an answer to the question, are you Christian. I cannot claim to be Christian, lest I be arrogant; I cannot reject the characterization, lest I deny Christ. Yet no question is more significant. Might an avenue around the paradox, then, be this, in which surely all of us will appreciate some cogency? If you wish to know whether I am Christian, perhaps you will not ask me but will ask any neighbor. You may ask my family; you may ask my children, or the children down the street. You may ask those under whom I work. You may ask those who work under me. Perhaps you will ask the widow and the fatherless. "By this shall men know that ye are my disciples, that ye love one another."

Yet which of us loves sufficiently to stand before that searching test? I said that you would appreciate the cogency of this. Yet do you not appreciate also the terror? I, at least, for one know that by this criterion I am lost. I myself know that I am not as Christian as I should be. You may summon my neighbors to witness, and they will expose me still further, will report on my failures even beyond my own penitent awareness, will strip from me the emperor's clothes of even my unconscious rationalizations. And yet . . . . Their accusation is important; but it is not the final answer. I am not Christian as I should be. Yet even so, God will not act on that, or none of us would escape whipping. I cower in fear—or would, except that Christ says to me, "Fear not. I have overcome the world." Are adjectives, then, so important after all? My adjectives are too thin and ragged to support me; and yet I do not fall, for Christ has shown me (I wrote this lecture on Good Friday) that God will Himself suffer rather than let me go. At one level, of course it matters what kind of person I am—matters to God, to me, and to the world. At the deepest level, however, the kind of person *I* am is just not good enough—not good enough to save me; and yet I have been saved. Not by my qualities, but by God's love.

At this level, yes, it is true that adjectives dissolve. For all dissolves, when we meet God face to face. Yet adjectives dissolve not to be replaced by nouns. Indeed, I am not saved by my virtues, by my qualifications, my adjectival status; for ultimately these are too utterly negligible. Yet it is a superficial and coldly formal theology that in such an extremity would suggest that I am being saved by being "a Christian": this is a back-door repetition of the very error that it is calculated to replace. It still surreptitiously suggests that something of *mine* justifies me; even if only my acceptance of salvation. I sometimes wonder whether even the idea of salvation by faith does not remain too anthropocentric, as if what brings us into God's presence were something that we do—having faith, becoming a Christian, or the like—rather than His anguish and His love. He loves us, not because of what we are, but regardless.

As we return to earth, then, from our encounter with that divine love, the quality of our life is the result of it, not the cause. I strive to be Christian, now, not in the hopes that if I succeed He will accept me; but in the knowledge, learned in Christ, that He *has* accepted me; and in glad response to His love. I strive to become as

Christian as I can, because His love constraineth me. It is to this that He inspires me. The adjectives are not my offering to Him, but His gift to me; a gift which I have the freedom and the honor to use. I strive to be as Christian as I can, because His love has shown me that this is important. I dare to say even, as does the Islamic theologian, that to be adjectivally *muslim* also is His gift, is man's response to His initiative.

I still hold, then, that there are no nouns. Religious life begins in the fact of God: a fact that includes His initiative, His agony, His love for all of us without exception, without discrimination, without favor, without remainder. Given that fact—and it is given; absolutely, and quite independently of whether or how we human beings recognize it; given that irremovable fact, religious life then consists in the *quality* of our response.

INDEX